Contents

Parts of a verb

When you learn a tense of a verb, you need to know how the verb changes for each **subject** (the person or thing 'doing' the verb). In order to have the same pattern for all verbs, the subjects are grouped as singular and plural and divided into the 1st, 2nd and 3rd 'persons'.

Here are the **subject pronouns** (used instead of a noun):

	singular	plural
1st person	je (j') *I*	nous *we*
2nd person	tu *you*	vous *you*
3rd person	il *he, it* elle *she, it* on *one, we*	ils *they* elles *they (all female)*

Notes:
- *je* is shortened to *j'* before a vowel or h.
- There are two words for 'you':
  tu is informal, used for one friend or young person;
  vous is formal, used for one adult (e.g. a teacher, a shop assistant);
  vous is used for more than one person, both formal and informal.
- *il* and *elle* mean 'he' and 'she', or when used for things they mean 'it'.
- *ils* and *elles* mean 'they'. Only use *elles* when **all** the nouns referred to are feminine.
- *on* can mean 'one', 'we', 'you', 'they', 'people in general'. The verb is always 3rd person singular, even when the meaning is plural (we, they, people). However, if you use *on est* + adjective, the adjective is usually plural:
  *On est différent**s***. People are different.

1 **Circle the correct pronoun in each sentence.**

   a Il y a un tournoi de tennis. **Il / Elle / Ils** est à Wimbledon.
   b Tu vois les volets? **Il / Elle / Ils** sont aux fenêtres.
   c Voici ma sœur. **Il / Elle / Ils** aime la Grande-Bretagne.
   d Au collège, moi, **je / tu / vous** porte un jean et un sweat.
   e Voici Lucile et Mélody. **Vous / Ils / Elles** sont dans ma classe.
   f Mes amis et moi, **elle / nous / vous** allons à Londres.

2 **Write the correct subject and verb in the gap in each sentence, choosing from the box. Then translate each sentence.**

> allez-vous   tu as   tu fais
> vous aimez   vous habitez

   a Salut, Maxime, qu'est-ce que _____? _____
   b Fabien et Zoë, quand _____ à Londres? _____
   c Monsieur, _____ visiter la Grande-Bretagne? _____
   d Maman, _____ mon passeport? _____
   e M. et Mme Lebrun, _____ dans un appartement? _____

3 **Draw lines to match the French to the English.**

   a On mange des croissants.   **1** They have a republic.
   b On roule à droite.   **2** You use the euro.
   c On porte un uniforme.   **3** People drive on the right.
   d On a une république.   **4** We're not very different.
   e On utilise l'euro.   **5** We like tennis.
   f On aime le tennis.   **6** They eat croissants.
   g On n'est pas très différents.   **7** We wear a uniform.

Negatives

To say somebody does <u>not</u> do something, you put *ne ... pas* around the verb – it's like the bread around a 'verb sandwich'. Shorten *ne* to *n'* before a vowel or h.
il prend (he takes) – *il **ne** prend **pas*** (he doesn't take)
j'aime (I like) – *je **n'**aime **pas*** (I don't like)

In the perfect tense, *ne ... pas* goes around the auxiliary verb (part of *avoir* or *être*).
j'ai regardé (I watched) – *je **n'**ai **pas** regardé* (I didn't watch)

Some other negative phrases use *ne (n')* in the same way:
- *ne ... rien* (nothing) *Il **ne** fait **rien**.* (He does nothing / doesn't do anything.)
- *ne ... jamais* (never) *Je **ne** prends **jamais** le bus.* (I never take the bus.)
- *ne ... ni ... ni ...* (neither ... nor) *Elle **ne** mange **ni** viande **ni** poisson.* (She eats neither meat nor fish.)
- *ne ... plus* (no more, no longer) *Il **ne** prend **plus** le train.* (He doesn't take the train any more / no longer takes the train.)

After a negative verb you usually put *de* (or *d'*) before a noun instead of *du/de la/des* or *un/une*.
*On **ne** porte **pas** d'uniforme.* *Tu **n'**as **jamais de** chocolat!*

1 **Are these sentences positive (P) or negative (N)?**
In the negative ones, underline all parts of the negative phrases.

a Je vais au collège en bus. ☐
b On ne roule pas à gauche en France. ☐
c Mon ami n'a jamais pris l'avion. ☐
d On a une monarchie en Grande-Bretagne. ☐
e On n'a rien fait hier soir. ☐

f Nous aimons les vacances sportives. ☐
g Tu vas en Écosse en vacances? ☐
h Elle ne va plus à la maison des jeunes. ☐
i Ça, c'est intéressant. ☐
j Il ne prend ni le train ni le bus. ☐

2 **Answer the questions, using the negative phrase suggested in brackets (and other words).**

a Tu prends le bus pour aller au collège?
Non, je _____ prends _____ le bus. (*not*)
b Tu utilises ton vélo?
Non, je _____ utilise _____ mon vélo. (*never*)
c Tu as regardé un film? Non, je _____ regardé de film. (*not*)
d Elle va à Paris ou à Nice?
Elle _____ ni à Paris _____ . (*neither ... nor*)
e On va en ville?
Non, on _____ . (*not any more*)
f Qu'est-ce que tu fais?
Je _____ . (*nothing*)

3 **Translate the sentences into French.**

a We're not going to Paris. _____
b My friend no longer goes on holiday. _____
c We're not doing anything this evening. _____
d She never takes the plane. _____
e He hasn't watched any films. _____
f I don't like the train or the bus. _____

Present tense of avoir

Here are all the parts of the present tense of *avoir* (to have). It does not follow the pattern of any other verb, so make sure you learn it. You will need to use it a lot, including to form the perfect tense of most verbs (see page 35).

j'ai	*nous avons*
tu as	*vous avez*
il/elle/on a	*ils/elles ont*

The verb *avoir* usually means 'have', but in some phrases it needs a different translation.
avoir (13) ans – to be (13) years old
avoir faim – to be hungry
avoir soif – to be thirsty
avoir besoin de – to need ('to have need of')
avoir peur de – to be afraid of
il y a – there is, there are

1 Underline the words which are part of *avoir*. Then draw lines to match the sentences to their translations.

1 Tu as de bonnes notes à l'école.
2 J'ai une grande collection de chansons.
3 Avez-vous voté pour les gadgets de votre top trois?
4 J'ai vu un très bon film.
5 Mon vieux portable a des touches.
6 Nous allons au café car nous avons faim.
7 Qu'est-ce qu'ils ont fait?
8 Il y a des volets aux fenêtres.

a My old mobile has buttons.
b What have they done?
c You have good marks at school.
d There are shutters at the windows.
e Have you voted for your top three gadgets?
f I saw a very good film.
g We're going to the café because we're hungry.
h I have a big collection of songs.

2 Circle the correct part of the verb *avoir* each time.

a
Dans ma chambre, j' **ai** / **as** / **a** beaucoup de gadgets.

b
Nous **avons** / **avez** / **ont** vu un documentaire sur Napoléon.

c
Tu **a** / **avez** / **as** toutes les BD de Tintin?

d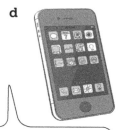
Il y **ai** / **a** / **ont** cinquante applis sur mon smartphone.

e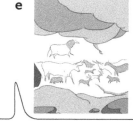
Les peintures de Lascaux **avons** / **avez** / **ont** plus de 17 000 ans!

3 Translate the sentences into French.

a I have a big collection of comic books. _____

b She is fourteen years old. _____

c We have lots of gadgets. _____

d You are thirsty. _____

e Have you seen the documentary? _____

f What has he done? _____

Grammar

Present tense of être

Here are all the parts of the present tense of *être*. It does not follow the pattern of any other verb, so make sure you learn it. You will need to use it a lot, including to form the perfect tense of some verbs (see page 37).

je suis	nous sommes
tu es	vous êtes
il/elle/on est	ils/elles sont

If you use an adjective after the verb *être*, it must agree with the subject of the sentence.

Il est grand.	**Ils** sont grand**s**.
Elle est grand**e**.	**Elles** sont grand**es**.

See page 16 for more practice of adjectives.

1 Complete the sentences with the correct phrase from the box.
Then translate the sentences.

a Les westerns, je ne _____

_____

b Où est-ce que tu _____

_____

c Le mont Blanc _____

_____

d Les frères Lumière _____

_____

e Mon frère et moi, nous _____

_____

f Est-ce que vous _____

_____

es née, Lucile?
est situé dans les Alpes.
êtes allés en Irlande?
sommes très différents.
sont des Français
  célèbres.
suis pas fan!

2 Use the completed crossword grid to help you number the clues correctly. Then write the correct words from the grid into each sentence.

Horizontalement

☐ J'aime la chanson parce que la mélodie _____ bonne.

☐ Non, je ne _____ pas d'accord!

☐ Les sentiments _____ modernes.

☐ Ma sœur et _____, nous sommes fans de rock.

Verticalement

☐ Alice, _____ es fan de musique classique?

☐ Zarah adore le nouvel album – _____ est fantastique.

☐ J'aime les romans comiques – _____ sont amusants.

☐ Nous _____ en vacances en Suisse.

☐ Vous _____ arrivés à quelle heure?

¹S	O	N	²T		
O			U		³Ê
⁴M	O	⁵I			T
M		L			E
E		⁶S	U	⁷I	S
⁸E	S	T		L	

Connectives join sentences together or make a sentence longer. This raises the level of your speaking and writing and makes your work more interesting, especially if you vary the ones you use.

et – and

mais – but

donc – so, therefore

comme – as (use at the start of a sentence)

car, parce que (*parce qu'* before a vowel) – because

par contre, en revanche – on the other hand

cependant, pourtant – however

1 **Underline the connectives in these sentences.**

a En France, on roule à droite mais en Grande-Bretagne, on roule à gauche.

b En France, on utilise l'euro. Cependant, en Grande-Bretagne, on utilise la livre sterling.

c On joue au cricket en Grande-Bretagne et on joue à la petanque en France.

d Il y a le tournoi de Wimbledon en Grande-Bretagne. Par contre, il y a le tournoi de Roland-Garros en France.

e Il y a beaucoup de différences. En revanche, il y a aussi beaucoup de similarités.

f Comme il y a juste la Manche qui nous sépare, nos pays ne sont pas si différents.

g Il y a des personnalités célèbres françaises, pourtant il y a aussi des personnalités importantes britanniques.

h Les différences sont intéressantes donc j'aime les deux pays!

2 **Find nine connectives in the wordsearch grid. Write them in the gaps in the text.**

J'aime beaucoup de BD, (**a**) _ _ _ _ _ _ _ _ _ _ _ _ ma BD préférée, c'est *Astérix le Gaulois*. Astérix est le personnage principal; il est petit (**b**) _ _ très intelligent. (**c**) _ _ _ _ _ _ _ _ _ _ _ , son ami Obélix est assez idiot, (**d**) _ _ _ _ _ il est aussi comique. Obélix a bu (= *drank*) une potion magique quand il était jeune (**e**) _ _ _ _ _ il est très, très fort. Les Romains sont les ennemis d'Astérix et Obélix, (**f**) _ _ _ les Gaulois se battent contre les Romains. (**g**) _ _ _ _ _ _ ils détestent les Romains, il y a beaucoup de bagarres (= *fights*). Les Gaulois aiment manger des sangliers (= *wild boar*), (**h**) _ _ _ _ _ _ _ _ _ ils sont délicieux. (**i**) _ _ _ _ _ _ _ _ _ _ _ _ _ , ils n'aiment pas les chansons du chanteur du village. Il ne chante pas bien!

A	C	E	C	G	P	I	L	N	P
E	N	R	E	V	A	N	C	H	E
R	S	U	P	X	R	Z	B	D	F
H	J	L	E	M	C	O	M	M	E
C	A	R	N	O	O	Q	T	W	Y
A	C	E	D	O	N	C	G	I	K
E	L	N	A	P	T	R	T	V	X
T	Z	B	N	D	R	M	A	I	S
F	H	J	T	L	E	N	P	R	T
V	X	P	A	R	C	E	Q	U	'

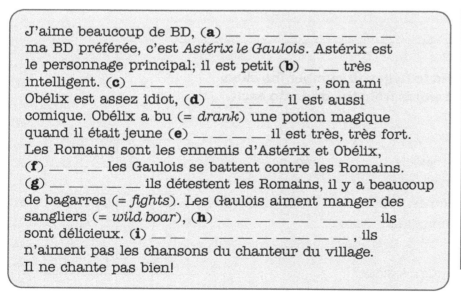

Connectives (2)

1 **Join the sentences using *qui*.**

  a C'est mon père. **Il** aime les comédies.

  _____

  b La France est un pays. **La France** utilise l'euro.

  _____

  c Marion Cotillard est une actrice française. **Elle** est née en 1975.

  _____

  d Lucky Luke est un cowboy imaginaire. **C'**est le personnage principal d'une BD.

  _____

  e Le capitaine Haddock est un personnage de BD. **Il** est le meilleur ami de Tintin.

  _____

2 **Join the sentences using *que*.**

  a Astérix est un personnage de BD. J'aime beaucoup **Astérix**.

  _____

  b J'ai un smartphone. J'adore **mon smartphone**.

  _____

  c *Les Misérables* est un livre. Victor Hugo a écrit **le livre**.

  _____

  d C'est un film. Je trouve **le film** ennuyeux.

  _____

  e Chez nous, il y a un uniforme. On porte **l'uniforme** à lécole.

  _____

3 **Say what these sentences mean in English.**

  a Ce qui est important, c'est le travail de Marie Curie sur la radioactivité.

  b Ce qui m'intéresse, c'est l'Histoire de France.

  c Ce que j'admire, c'est le style de Jean-Paul Gaultier.

  d Ce que je déteste, c'est la musique électronique.

4 **Complete the sentences in your own way.**

  a Ce qui est important, c'est _____

  b Ce qui m'intéresse, c'est _____

  c Ce que j'admire, c'est _____

  d Ce que je déteste, c'est _____

The relative pronouns *qui* and *que* mean 'who', 'which' or 'that'.

qui stands in for the **subject** of a verb, so it is usually followed by a verb.
*Louis Blériot était un pilote français. **Il** a traversé la Manche en avion en 1909.*
→ *Louis Blériot était un pilote français **qui** a traversé la Manche en avion en 1909.*
(Louis Blériot was a French pilot **who** flew across the Channel in 1909.)

que stands in for the **object** of a verb, so it is usually followed by a noun or pronoun.
Tintin est une BD. J'aime **Tintin**.
→ *Tintin est une BD **que** j'aime.*
(*Tintin* is a comic book **that** I like.)
Shorten *que* to *qu'* before a vowel (e.g. *il, elle, on*).

---

ce qui and *ce que* mean 'what' or 'the thing that'. They are often used at the beginning of a sentence to emphasise something.

Use *ce qui* as the **subject** of a verb and *ce que* (*ce qu'*) as the **object**.
La pop (subject) *est vraiment cool.*
→ ***Ce qui** est vraiment cool, c'est la pop.* (**What** is really cool is pop music.)
*J'adore **la pop*** (object).
→ ***Ce que** j'adore, c'est la pop.* (**The thing (that)** I love is pop music.)

There are different ways to ask a question in French. For example, to ask 'Do you like comedies?', you can:
- simply add a question mark to a statement and make your voice rise at the end
  Tu aimes *les comédies?*
- add *Est-ce que ...* at the beginning
  Est-ce que tu aimes *les comédies?*
- turn the subject and verb round and add a hyphen (this is called inversion)
  Aimes-tu *les comédies?*
  In the perfect tense, the auxiliary verb (part of *avoir* or *être*) is the part that is turned round.
  As-tu *visité Paris?* (Did you visit Paris?)
  Est-il *arrivé à la gare?* (Has he arrived at the station?)

Sometimes you need to add a question word.

Qu'est-ce que ...? (What ...?) does not need inversion:
Qu'est-ce que **tu aimes**? (What do you like?)

With other question words you usually need inversion:
Où **travailles-tu**? (Where do you work?)
Quand **es-tu** *allé à Paris?* (When did you go to Paris?)

Here are some more question words:
combien? – how much?
comment? – how? what like?
pourquoi? – why?
qui? – who?
quel / quelle / quels / quelles ...? – which ...? what ...?

1 **Make these statements into questions using *Est-ce que*, then translate them into English.**

a Tu fais du sport. _____ _____

b Tu parles espagnol. _____ _____

c Léa aime manger les fruits. _____ _____

d Vous avez travaillé en France. _____ _____

2 **Make these statements into questions using inversion, then translate them into English. Remember the hyphen.**

a Tu aimes ton travail. _____ _____

b Vous avez de l'argent. _____ _____

c Tu dois passer un examen. _____ _____

d Tu as étudié les sciences. _____ _____

3 **Write out each question correctly. Then find the English meaning below and write its number in the box.**

a les légumes / tu / Est-ce que / aimes / ? _____ ☐

b elle / Qu'est-ce qu' / inventé / a / ? _____ ☐

c parler / Dois / langues / d'autres / -tu / ? _____ ☐

d faire / vas-tu / études / Quelles / ? _____ ☐

e ce travail / as / commencé / -tu / Quand / ? _____ ☐

f as / ce métier / Pourquoi / -tu / choisi / ? _____ ☐

> **1** Do you have to speak other languages?
> **2** Why did you choose this job?
> **3** Do you like vegetables?
> **4** When did you start this work?
> **5** What studies are you going to do?
> **6** What did she invent?

The **direct object pronouns** that mean 'him', 'her', 'it' and 'them' look the same as the words for 'the'. They are placed before the verb.
- *le* refers to masculine nouns (him, it) ⎤
- *la* refers to feminine nouns (her, it) ⎬ *le* and *la* become *l'* before a vowel or h
- *les* refers to plural nouns ⎦

Le film, je **le** trouve cool.
La mélodie, je **la** trouve triste.
Le chanteur, je **l'**adore.
Les documentaires? Je **les** déteste!

In the perfect tense the direct object pronoun goes before the auxiliary verb (part of *avoir* or *être*).
*Je **l'**ai aimé.* (I liked it.)

In the negative, *ne … pas* goes round the pronoun and the verb.
*Je ne **les** aime pas.* (I don't like them.)
*Je ne **l'**ai pas aimé.* (I didn't like it.)

1 Circle the direct object pronouns in this text.

> Moi, j'aime les dessins animés parce que je les trouve amusants. En revanche, les émissions de télé-réalité, je les trouve bêtes. Je préfère la musique, surtout le hip-hop. Ah oui, ce genre de musique, je l'adore. Les magazines? Je ne les lis pas souvent, mais j'aime lire des romans. La série *Oksa Pollock* est fantastique – je l'aime bien. Le dernier livre de cette série, je le lis en ce moment.

TIP

Watch out – *le, la, l'* and *les* can also be articles (meaning 'the'), so you need to work out which ones in the text are direct object pronouns.

2 Write the correct pronoun in the gap in each sentence.

a Les jeux télévisés, je _____ aime bien.

b J'adore la musique, je _____ trouve passionnante.

c Les bandes dessinées, je _____ adore.

d Par contre, le personnage principal, je _____ déteste.

e J'ai commencé le livre, mais je ne _____ ai pas fini.

f Le film était assez long mais je _____ ai aimé.

3 Complete the sentences as you wish, but you must use a direct object pronoun.

a Les émissions musicales? Je _____

b Tu aimes la musique classique? _____

c Cette chanteuse, je _____

d Tu as aimé le film? _____

4 Translate these sentences into English.

a Je te trouve très calme. _____

b Les comédies nous amusent. _____

c Mes parents me traitent comme un bébé. _____

d Léa et Max, je vous attends au café. _____

Here are more pronouns that also go in front of the verb:
me/m'	me	*nous*	us
te/t'	you	*vous*	you

(See also: page 12 Indirect object pronouns, page 28 Reflexive verbs.)

Indirect object pronouns

Indirect object pronouns are mostly used to replace nouns that have *à* before them.

singular		plural	
me	(to) me	*nous*	(to) us
te	(to) you	*vous*	(to) you
lui	(to) him/her	*leur*	(to) them

They go before the verb, as do other object pronouns in French.

*Je téléphone **à ma copine**.* → *Je **lui** téléphone.*
(I phone **my friend**. → I phone **her**.)
*Il a parlé **à ses parents**.* → *Il **leur** a parlé.*
(He spoke **to his parents**. → He spoke to **them**.)

In the negative, *ne ... pas* goes round the pronoun and the verb.
*Ils ne **m'**ont pas écrit.* (They didn't write to me.)

Here are some verbs that are used with indirect object pronouns:
demander à – to ask
dire à – to say (to)
donner à – to give (to)
écrire à – to write to
envoyer à – to send to
faire confiance à – to trust
parler à – to speak to
téléphoner à – to phone

1 Underline the indirect object pronouns in the French sentences, then draw lines to match them to the English.

a Ma mère me donne 20 euros.
b Je te parle de mon travail.
c Florian lui téléphone ce soir.
d Tu leur as écrit?
e Je lui ai demandé de rester ici.
f Elle vous a envoyé des SMS?
g Ils nous ont téléphoné hier.
h Mon père ne me fait pas confiance.

1 Have you written to them?
2 Has she sent you some texts?
3 I'll talk to you about my work.
4 My father doesn't trust me.
5 My mother gives me 20 euros.
6 They phoned us yesterday.
7 I've asked him to stay here.
8 Florian is phoning her this evening.

2 Rewrite each sentence, replacing the underlined part with an indirect object pronoun in the correct place.

a Elle parle <u>à son meilleur ami</u>. _____

b Nous donnons 10 euros <u>à Laura</u>. _____

c J'ai envoyé des SMS <u>à ma copine</u>. _____

d Je n'ai pas téléphone <u>à mes parents</u>. _____

e Ils font confiance <u>à mon frère</u>. _____

3 Answer the questions as you wish, but you must use indirect object pronouns.

a Tu téléphones souvent à tes parents? _____

b Qu'est-ce que tu as dit à ton prof? _____

c Qui t'a donné de l'argent? _____

d Tes parents te font confiance? _____

e Tu envoies combien de SMS à tes amis par jour? _____

Grammar

Opinions (present tense)

To say what you like and don't like, use:
- *j'adore* ... ☺☺
- *j'aime* ... / *j'aime bien* ... ☺
- *ça dépend* 😐
- *je n'aime pas* ... ☹
- *je déteste* ... / *j'ai horreur de* ... ☹☹

Use the verbs with nouns and pronouns:
- *J'aime* **les documentaires**.
- ***La musique**, j'aime* **ça**.
- ***Cette émission**, je* **la** *déteste!*

Or use them with verbs in the infinitive:
- *J'aime* ***regarder*** *des films.*

It is important to give reasons for your opinion. Use these phrases:
- *parce que* / *car* (because)
- *c'est* (it is) + adjective
- *je pense/trouve que c'est* ... (I think/find it is ...)
- *je le/la/les trouve* + adjective (I find it/them ...)

If you don't like something you can add *je préfère* ... and name something else.

1 Are these opinions positive (P) or negative (N)?

- **a** Les comédies, j'aime ça. ☐
- **b** J'adore le rock. ☐
- **c** Je n'aime pas regarder la télé. ☐
- **d** Les séries, ça dépend... mais en général elles sont ennuyeuses. ☐
- **e** Les informations, c'est déprimant. ☐
- **f** J'aime chanter quand il y a une émission musicale. ☐
- **g** J'aime la musique punk. C'est passionnant. ☐
- **h** La musique classique? J'ai horreur de ça. ☐

2 Rewrite these sentences so that they include a second verb in the infinitive. Choose from: *écouter*, *regarder* and *lire*.

- **a** J'adore les jeux télévisés. ____________________
- **b** Je n'aime pas la musique punk. ____________________
- **c** Je déteste les romans historiques. ____________________
- **d** Tu aimes les BD? ____________________

3 Choose four of the items below and give your opinion, with a reason. Adapt phrases from exercises 1 and 2 where possible.

____

____

____

____

a 

b 

c 

d 

e 

f 

Sometimes you need to give opinions in different tenses.

Perfect	j'ai il/elle/on a	adoré aimé détesté préféré trouvé	I he/she/we	loved liked hated preferred found	The expressions *c'était*, *c'est* and *ce sera* are all from the verb *être* (to be).
Imperfect	c'était	+ adjective	it was		
	c'est	+ adjective	it is		
Present	je/j' il/elle/on	adore aime déteste préfère trouve	I he/she/we	love like hate prefer find	
Future	ce sera	+ adjective	it will be		

1 **Draw lines to match the French to the English**

a J'aime utiliser mon vélo. C'est moins polluant.
b Je déteste prendre le bus, je préfère le train.
c Je vais à un concert de rock. Ce sera génial.
d Olivier a préféré regarder la télé.
e Je n'ai pas aimé le film – il était vraiment nul.
f Je trouve que la chanteuse était incroyable!
g On a trouvé le match un peu ennuyeux.
h Je ne suis pas d'accord. À mon avis c'était excitant.

1 I didn't like the film – it was really rubbish.
2 I'm going to a rock concert. It'll be great.
3 We found the match a bit boring.
4 I hate taking the bus, I prefer the train.
5 I don't agree. In my opinion it was exciting.
6 I like using my bike. It's less polluting.
7 I think the singer was incredible!
8 Olivier preferred to watch TV.

2 **Which tenses are used in exercise 1? Fill in the grid with the letter of each French sentence. Watch out – some sentences have more than one tense!**

Perfect	Imperfect	Present	Future
		a,	

3 **Complete each sentence with the correct form of the verb, then translate into English.**

a J'ai lu ce livre deux fois parce que je l'_____ captivant. (**trouver** – *perfect*)
_____

b Il ne prend pas le train parce qu'il _____ voyager en bus. (**préférer** – *present*)
_____

c Elle _____ le concert. C'_____ nul. (**détester** – *perfect*, **être** – *imperfect*)
_____

d On va en Suisse – ce _____ vraiment incroyable. (**être** – *future*)
_____

e Salomé n' _____ pas _____ le documentaire. Moi non plus. (**aimer** – *perfect*)
_____

faire + infinitive

To say that something makes you dance (or whatever), use *ça me fait* ... with a verb in the **infinitive**. Remember that the pronoun *me* goes before the verb *faire*, not before the infinitive.
*Ça me fait **danser**.* (That makes me dance.)
Other infinitives you could use with this expression:
dormir (to sleep), *rêver* (to dream), *pleurer* (to cry), *rire* (to laugh), *vomir* (to be sick).

Beware! If you want to say that something makes you happy (etc.), use *ça me rend* ... with an **adjective**.
*Ça me rend **heureux/heureuse**.* (That makes me happy.)
If *me* refers to a female, the adjective must be feminine (*heureuse*).
Other adjectives you could use with this expression:
triste (sad), *fou/folle* (crazy), *malade* (ill)

1 Find the correct caption for each picture and write the number in the box.

a

b

c

d

e

f

1 J'adore écouter la musique de Mozart. Ça me fait dormir.
2 Moi, j'écoute du reggae – ça me fait rêver.
3 J'aime écouter des chansons tristes mais ça me fait pleurer.
4 Je n'aime pas regarder les films romantiques. Ça me fait vomir!
5 Je lis beaucoup de BD, ça me fait rire.
6 J'adore le rythme du rock, ça me fait danser.

2 Which pictures in exercise 1 fit these captions? Write the correct letter.

1 Ça me rend triste.
2 Ça me rend malade.
3 Ça me rend fou.
4 Ça me rend heureux.
5 Ça me rend heureuse.
6 Ça me rend paresseuse.

3 Adapt the sentences to say three things about yourself using *ça me fait* and *ça me rend*.

a _____

b _____

c _____

TIP

Once you have mastered these expressions, try using them in the past as well:
*Ça m'**a fait** rire.* (It **made** me laugh.)
*Le film m'**a rendu** triste.* (The film **made** me sad.)

Adjectives (agreement)

Adjectives have to 'agree' with the nouns (people, places, things) they describe. They do this by changing their spelling for feminine and plural.

- Most adjectives add **-e** for feminine and **-s** for plural.
- Adjectives ending in **-e** (no accent) do not add an extra **-e** for feminine.
- Adjectives ending in **-s** do not add an extra **-s** for masculine plural.
- Adjectives ending in **-el** have **-elle** in the feminine.
- The colours *orange* and *marron* do not change at all.
- Some adjectives have a slightly different pattern from normal, as shown in the grid.

singular		plural	
masc.	fem.	masc.	fem.
-eur	**-euse**	-eurs	**-euses**
-eux	**-euse**	-eux	**-euses**
-if	**-ive**	-ifs	**-ives**

1 Complete the table.

masculine singular	feminine singular	masculine plural	feminine plural	English meaning
démodé	démodée			*old-fashioned*
divertissant			divertissantes	*entertaining*
	éducative			
enfantin		enfantins		
ennuyeux			ennuyeuses	
	essentielle			
gris			grises	
rapide	rapide			

2 Circle the correct form of the adjective.

a J'aime les jeux parce qu'ils sont **amusante / amusants**.

b J'adore la musique parce que je la trouve **divertissante / divertissants**.

c Les documentaires sont toujours très **informative / informatifs**.

d Je n'aime pas mon portable **bleu / bleue** parce qu'il est **démodé / démodées**.

e Les gadgets **pratique / pratiques** sont souvent trop **ennuyeux / ennuyeuse**.

TIP

Look for words in each sentence that help you know whether a noun is masculine or feminine, singular or plural, e.g. *le/la/les, un/une/des, mon/ma/ mes, il/elle/ils/elles,* or other adjectives.

3 Complete the sentences with the correct form of the adjective.

a J'adore les tablettes – elles sont _____ . (**essentiel**)

b Je regarde la télé – c'est une émission _____ . (**éducatif**)

c À mon avis, les émissions musicales sont _____ . (**passionnant**)

d Tu aimes les informations? Non, elles sont _____ . (**nul**)

e Ma copine est _____ mais ses frères ne sont pas du tout _____ . (**travailleur**)

Most adjectives follow the noun, but a few common ones go **before** the noun (as in English). Here are some (with the feminine form in brackets):
petit(e), grand(e), gros(se) – little, big
joli(e), gentil(le) – pretty, kind
bon(ne), mauvais(e) – good, bad
*jeune, *vieux* – young, old
**beau, *nouveau* – beautiful, new

* The last three adjectives in this list do not follow the usual pattern of agreement.

	singular			plural	
masc.	**masc. before vowel or silent h**	**fem.**	**masc.**	**fem.**
vieux	vieil	vieille	vieux	vieilles
beau	bel	belle	beaux	belles
nouveau	nouvel	nouvelle	nouveaux	nouvelles

1 Complete the sentences with the correct form of the adjectives.

a Je n'aime pas mon _____ portable. (*old*)

b Léo est un _____ garçon. (*kind*)

c Je préfère les _____ films. (*old*)

d Je déteste la _____ tablette _____. (*old, green*)

e Tu as vu mes _____ baskets _____? (*new, blue*)

f J'ai une _____ _____ chambre. (*beautiful, little*)

g J'adore mon _____ ordinateur. (*beautiful*)

h C'est un _____ appartement _____. (*big, modern*)

> **TIP**
>
> *basket* is feminine.

2 Write the sentences in the correct order, with the adjective in the right place. (Watch out – some go before, some after the noun.)

a rouge / aime / nouvelle / la / J' / tablette / . _____

b n' / les / pas / aime / gris / vieux / Je / ordinateurs / . _____

c gros / Elle / noir / a / chien / un / . _____

d mes / aimes / jeux vidéo / nouveaux / Tu / ? _____

e tablette / vieille / a / petit / Ma / écran / un / . _____

3 Complete the sentences.

a Je n'aime pas le nouvel ordinateur. Je préfère _____ .
(*the old one*)

b J'aime la vieille console mais j'adore _____ . (*the new one*)

c Je déteste les gros chiens, je préfère _____ . (*the little ones*)

d Je n'aime pas les baskets blanches, je préfère _____ .
(*the green ones*)

> Some adjectives can be used as nouns – just add *le/la/les* and the correct adjective ending.
> *le nouveau* (the new one)
> *les grands* (the big ones)
> *la vieille* (the old one)
> *les bonnes* (the good ones)

4 Match the French to the English.

a la vieille

b les jeunes

c le petit

1 young people

2 the little boy

3 the old lady

Comparative and superlative ▶ *Allez 2 Student Book* **1.2, 7.1**

1 **Look at the map and read the statements. Write true (T) or false (F).**

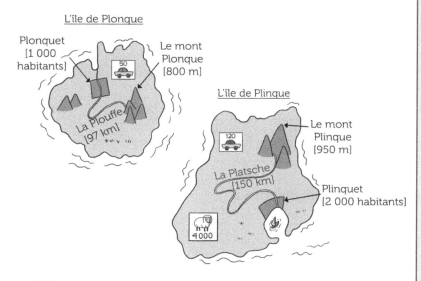

L'île de Plonque

Plonquet [1 000 habitants]

Le mont Plonque [800 m]

La Plouffe [97 km]

L'île de Plinque

Le mont Plinque [950 m]

La Platsche [150 km]

Plinquet [2 000 habitants]

4 000

a ☐ L'île de Plinque est plus grande que l'île de Plonque.

b ☐ Le mont Plonque est moins haut que le mont Plinque.

c ☐ Plinquet est deux fois plus peuplée que Plonquet.

d ☐ Les voitures sont plus nombreuses sur l'île de Plonque.

e ☐ À Plinquet les moutons sont aussi nombreux que les habitants.

f ☐ La Plouffe est plus longue que la Platsche.

> To make comparisons, put *plus* (more) or *moins* (less) before an adjective and follow it with *que* (than). Use *aussi ... que* to say 'as ... as'.
>
> Remember to make the adjective agree with the first thing you are comparing. **La Loire** est <u>plus</u> long**ue** <u>que</u> la Seine. (The Loire is long<u>er than</u> the Seine.) **Les Pyrénées** sont <u>aussi</u> intéressant**es** <u>que</u> les Alpes. (The Pyrenees are <u>as</u> interesting <u>as</u> the Alps.)
>
> There are two irregular comparatives: *meilleur(e) que* (better than) *pire que* (worse than)
>
> Use the superlative to say that something is 'the most ...' or 'the least ...'.
>
> | le
la
les | plus (*most*)
moins (*least*) | + adjective |
> | --- | --- | --- |
> | | meilleur(e)(s) (*best*)
pire(s) (*worst*) | |
>
> *C'est* **le** *moyen de transport* **le moins cher**. (It's the least expensive/the cheapest means of transport.)

2 **Circle the correct adjective.**

a Le train est aussi **pratique / pratiques** que le car.

b Les avions sont plus **polluante / polluants** que les bateaux.

c Le métro et le bus sont moins **chère / chers** que le taxi.

d Le vélo est le **meilleur / meilleure** moyen de transport en ville.

e Les voitures sont les plus **dangereux /dangereuses**.

3 **Write two sentences comparing the islands in exercise 1. Then add some sentences of your own using comparatives and superlatives.**

_____

_____

_____

_____

_____

(For more practice of adjectives, see pages 16–17.)

The demonstrative adjectives (this/that, these/those) are used with nouns. In French, they have to match the gender and number of the noun, just like the words for 'the', 'my', 'your', etc.

singular (this, that)			plural (these, those)
masc.	masc. before vowel / silent h	fem.	
ce portable	**cet** ordinateur	**cette** tablette	**ces** smartphones

Watch out for the masculine singular form *cet* – it is only used when the next word begins with a vowel or silent h, e.g. **cet** *ordinateur* (that computer), **cet** *homme* (this man).
Look what happens if you add an adjective before the noun:
ce *petit ordinateur* (that little computer), **ce** *grand homme* (this great man)
The adjectives *petit* and *grand* doesn't begin with a vowel, so you use *ce* instead of *cet*.

1 Circle the correct demonstrative adjective in each sentence.

a   J'ai trouvé **ce** / **cette** / **ces** livres dans ma chambre.

b   J'ai acheté **ce** / **cet** / **cette** appareil photo, il est super.

c   Je préfère **ce** / **cette** / **ces** console de jeux.

d   Je trouve **ce** / **cet** / **cette** grand écran tactile très pratique.

e   Je n'aime pas **ce** / **cette** / **ces** touches, elles sont démodées.

f   Tu aimes **ce** / **cet** / **cette** appli? Elle n'est pas chère.

2 Complete the sentences with the correct form of *ce*.

a   Nous passons nos vacances dans _____ belle caravane.

b   J'habite dans _____ igloo, il est très confortable.

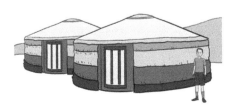

c   J'ai acheté _____ yourtes en Mongolie. Je les adore.

d   Ma famille habite dans _____ grand appartement.

> **TIP**
>
> If you're not sure whether a noun in exercises 1 and 2 is masculine or feminine, singular or plural, look for clues in the rest of the sentence. What does any adjective ending tell you? Are there any articles or pronouns (*le/la/les, il/elle, ils/elles*) to help you?
>
> Get used to looking for clues. You can also apply this strategy when deciding which possessive adjective to use (*mon/ma/mes, ton/ta/tes, son/sa/ses*).

Impersonal structures

► *Allez 2 Student Book* **3.3, 3.6, 5.1**

Use impersonal structures to say that **it is** important (or essential, difficult, etc.) **to do** something.
In French, most of these expressions follow the pattern *il est important (essentiel, difficile, etc.) de/d'* + infinitive.
Il est important **de** *boire assez d'eau.* (It is important to drink enough water.)

Negative expressions go before the infinitive and are not split up.
Il est important de **ne pas** *manger trop de produits sucrés.* (It is important not to eat too many sweet things.)
Il est difficile de **ne jamais** *faire de fautes.* (It's difficult to never make mistakes.)

To say what you must do or have to do, use the impersonal structure *il faut* + infinitive (no need for *de* this time).
Il faut manger des fruits. (You must eat fruit.)

Negatives go round the verb as normal.
Il **ne faut** *jamais* *donner ton adresse.* (You must **never** give your address.)

1 Match the French to the English.

a Il est important d'écouter attentivement.
b Il est nécessaire de regarder les informations.
c Il est difficile de ne pas parler en classe.
d Il est impossible de ne rien acheter en ville.
e Il est essentiel d'avoir beaucoup de vêtements.
f Il faut faire du sport régulièrement.
g Il ne faut pas passer trop de temps en ligne.
h Il ne faut jamais oublier son mot de passe.

1 You must do sport regularly.
2 It's impossible not to buy anything in town.
3 You must never forget your password.
4 It's important to listen carefully.
5 You must not spend too much time online.
6 It is necessary to watch the news.
7 It is essential to have lots of clothes.
8 It's difficult not to talk in class.

2 Translate the sentences into French.

a It is necessary to drink water _____

b It is difficult to listen regularly. _____

c It is essential not to forget your password. _____

d It is impossible to eat too many sweet things! _____

e You must speak French in class. _____

f You must not forget anything. _____

3 Complete these sentences as you wish.

a Il est impossible de _____

b Il faut _____

c Il est difficile de _____

d Il ne faut jamais _____

Grammar

Prepositions

Prepositions tell you something about one noun's relation to another.

à – to, at	*dans* – in	*à côté de* – next to
de – from, of	*entre* – between	*en face de* – opposite
sur – on	*devant* – in front of	*à droite de* – to the right of
sous – under	*derrière* – behind	*à gauche de* – to the left of

When you use *à* or *de* with a masculine or plural noun, they combine with the words for 'the'.

preposition	masculine noun	plural noun
à	à + le = **au** **au** cinéma	à + les = **aux** **aux** magasins
de	de + le = **du** **du** cinéma	de + les = **des** **des** magasins

1 **Underline all the prepositions and fill the gaps with the correct form of *à* or *de* and the definite article. Then translate the text into English.**

J'habite dans un appartement (**a**) _____ centre de notre village, en face (**b**) _____ magasins. Je vais (**c**) _____ magasins assez souvent. Notre appartement est (**d**) _____ rez-de-chaussée. Ma chambre est à gauche (**e**) _____ WC et en face (**f**) _____ salle de bains. C'est très pratique le matin! Dans ma chambre, le lit est à côté (**g**) _____ fenêtre. Sur la table, à droite (**h**) _____ étagère, il y a mon ordinateur. Je n'ai pas de télé.

Some verbs that are followed by an infinitive need the preposition *à* or *de* before the infinitive.

je passe du temps/une heure/...			*I spend time/an hour/... (doing)*
je commence / j'ai commencé	*à*		*I'm beginning / I began to*
je continue / j'ai continué			*I continue / I continued to*
il m'aide / il m'a aidé		*+ infinitive*	*he helps / he helped me to*
j'essaie / j'ai essayé			*I try / I tried to*
j'arrête / j'ai arrêté	*de*		*I'm stopping / I stopped (doing)*
ça me permet			*that allows me to*
il est important/impossible/...*			*it's important/impossible/... to*

(*See page 20 for practice of impersonal structures.)

TIP

If you're not sure, check the gender of a noun in the glossary or a dictionary. If a noun is plural or begins with a vowel, you don't need to know the gender for this exercise.

2 **Complete the sentences with the words from the box.**

a J'ai essayé _____ mon temps en ligne mais c'est difficile.

b Je commence _____ sur les réseaux sociaux.

c J'ai arrêté _____ aux jeux vidéo le soir.

d Je passe trop de temps _____ de la musique en ligne.

e J'aime les appels vidéo. Ça me permet _____ en contact avec mon grand-père.

f Mon frère m'a aidé _____ une tablette.

à aller	de jouer
à choisir	de limiter
à écouter	de rester

Pronouns (en, y)

► Allez 2 Student Book **5.2, 5.6, 8.1**

Use the pronoun *en* to replace a noun preceded by *du/de la/de l'/des* or by an expression of quantity.
It means 'of them', 'of it', 'some' or 'any'.
Like all pronouns, it comes before the verb.
In English we often miss out 'of it/them', but not in French.
*Tu manges **des légumes**? → Oui, j'**en** mange beaucoup.*
(Do you eat vegetables? → Yes, I eat lots (of them).)
*Tu fais **du sport**? → Non, je n'**en** fais pas.*
(Do you do any sport? → No, I don't do any.)
*Tu as acheté **de la viande**? → Non, je n'**en** ai pas acheté.*
(Did you buy some meat? → No, I didn't buy any.)

The pronoun *y* replaces a noun preceded by *à*.
It usually means 'there'.
*Je vais **à l'école**. → J'**y** vais.*
(I go to school. → I go there.)

The most common use is in the phrase *il y a* (there is/there are).

Notice the word order when you use *en* with *il y a*:
*Il y **en** a dix.* (There are ten (of them).)

1 **Write the answers correctly.**

   a Tu manges des fruits et des légumes?

   j' / Oui, / cinq / mange / en / par / jour / . ____Oui,_____

   b Tu as assez d'argent?

   assez / en / j' / Oui, / ai / . _____

   c Tu fais de la danse?

   fais / je / Non, / en / n' / pas /. _____

   d Tu as bu beaucoup de coca aujourd'hui?

   litre / j' / bu / Oui, / ai / en / un / . _____

   e Il y a des pommes?

   la / table / il / Oui, / en / trois / a / sur / y / . _____

   f Tu vas au supermarché demain?

   y / pas / n' / Non, / vais / je / . _____

2 **Look at the shopping basket and answer the questions using *en*.**

   a Il y a du pain? _____

   b Il y a combien de bouteilles? _____

   c Il y a six yaourts? _____

   d Tu as trouvé des céréales? _____

   e Tu as acheté des bananes? _____

3 **Make up two more questions and answers about the shopping basket.**

   f _____

   _____

   g _____

   _____

(See also: page 4 Parts of a verb, page 11 Direct object pronouns, page 12 Indirect object pronouns.)

Expressions of frequency

Use expressions of frequency to say how often you do something. (These are adverbs or adverbial phrases.) Watch out – in English some of these expressions are placed before the verb, but they must go after the verb in French.

Je **vais souvent** au café. (I **often go** to the café.)

To say 'never', use *ne ... jamais* around the verb.
Je **ne** vais **jamais** au café. (I never go to the café.)
(For practice of negative expressions, see page 5.)

1 Match up the frequency expressions in the grid (2–7) with their meanings in English. Then use the extra letters to complete the one down the centre of the grid.

a ☐ sometimes
b ☐ always
c [1] every day
d ☐ every week
e ☐ often
f ☐ regularly
g ☐ twice a day

```
                              1
       2  S  O  U  V  E  N  T
       3  Q  U  E  L  Q  U  E  F  O  I  S

       4  R  É  G  U  L  I  È  R  E  M  E  N  T
    5  T  O  U  T  E  S     L  E  S     S  E  M  A  I  N  E  S

       6  D  E  U  X     F  O  I  S     P  A  R     J  O  U  R

       7  T  O  U  J  O  U  R  S
```

E₁ J₈ O₁
S₁ S₁ U₁

2 Draw lines to match the sentence parts. Then translate the sentences.

a Je vais très souvent
b Il est important de boire
c Quelquefois, nous faisons
d En hiver, je fais du
e Il faut manger au moins
f Au petit déjeuner, je

1 de la natation.
2 cinq fruits et légumes par jour.
3 au centre sportif.
4 mange toujours des céréales.
5 ski une fois par semaine.
6 de l'eau régulièrement.

a _____
b _____
c _____
d _____
e _____
f _____

3 Write sentences to say what you do for your health. Include an expression of frequency in each one.

_____
_____
_____

Reflexive verbs

Reflexive verbs include a word for 'myself', 'yourself', 'himself', etc. This reflexive pronoun is not always used in English but it has to be there in French.

se protéger – *to protect yourself*		s'appeler – *to be called* (*'to call yourself'*)	
je **me** protège	*I protect myself*	je **m'**appelle	*me, te* and *se*
tu **te** protèges	*you protect yourself*	tu **t'**appelles	are shortened
il/elle **se** protège	*he/she protects himself/herself*	il/elle **s'**appelle	before a vowel or h
nous **nous** protégeons	*we protect ourselves*	nous **nous** appelons	
vous **vous** protégez	*you protect yourself/yourselves*	vous **vous** appelez	
ils/elles **se** protègent	*they protect themselves*	ils/elles **s'**appellent	

In the negative, *ne ... pas* (not) and *ne ... jamais* (never) go round the pronoun and verb together:
*Je **ne** m'habille **pas**.* (I don't get dressed.)
*Il **ne** s'amuse **jamais**.* (He never has fun.)

Learn these useful questions that contain the reflexive verb *se passer*:
Qu'est-ce qui se passe? (What is happening?)
Qu'est-ce qui s'est passé? (What (has) happened?)

1 Draw lines to match the French to the English.

a	se séparer de	**1**	to happen
b	se divertir	**2**	to sign up for
c	se passer	**3**	to be entertained
d	s'amuser	**4**	to get up
e	se lever	**5**	to be inspired by
f	se préparer	**6**	to be separated from
g	s'inscrire à	**7**	to be prepared
h	s'inspirer de	**8**	to make fun of
i	se moquer de	**9**	to have fun

TIP

In a dictionary or glossary, reflexive verbs are always shown in the infinitive with *se* or *s'*. But when used in a sentence as in exercise 2, **i**, and **j**, the infinitive needs a reflexive pronoun matching the subject of the sentence.
Je *vais **me lever** à sept heures.* (I am going to get (myself) up at 7 o'clock.) (Not: *se lever*)

2 Write the correct reflexive pronoun.

a Je _____ inscris au club de foot.

b Elle _____ inspire d'Angelina Jolie.

c Tu _____ prépares pour le déménagement?

d Ils _____ amusent à la fête.

e Comment vous _____ appelez?

f Nous _____ levons à six heures.

g Ces livres _____ moquent de la société française.

h Je _____ protège en ligne parce que ...

i ... je veux _____ divertir sans risques.

j Il ne peut pas _____ séparer de son smartphone.

3 Translate the sentences into French.

a We're having fun. _____

b I'm inspired by (+ name of your choice). _____

c She's getting ready for the party. _____

d I want to protect myself online. _____

e I don't want to be parted from my phone. _____

Present tense of –er verbs

Most French verbs end in *-er* in the infinitive.
To form the present tense, take *-er* off the infinitive
(e.g. *aimer → aim-*).
Add the following endings:

je ____**e**	nous ____**ons**
tu ____**es**	vous ____**ez**
il/elle/on ____**e**	ils/elles ____**ent**

The only exception, for *-er* verbs, is *aller* (to go)
– see pages 29 and 33.

Verbs like *manger* and *protéger* add an extra 'e' in the
nous form: *nous mangeons, nous protégeons*. This is
to make the g 'soft' (like 'j'), not 'hard' (as in 'golf').
For similar reasons, *commencer* (to begin) adds a
cedilla to the c (ç) in the *nous* form, to keep the soft
'c' sound: *nous commençons*.

The *-e/-es/-ent* endings are not sounded, so all parts
sound the same except for the *nous* and *vous* forms.

A few verbs have slight changes before the endings
that are not sounded:

- *préférer, répéter, protéger* and *compléter*
  change é to è
  je préfère, tu répètes, il protège, elle complète
  (but *nous préférons, vous répétez, vous protégez,
  nous complétons*)
- *acheter* changes e to è
  j'achète, ils achètent (but *vous achetez*).
- *appeler* has a double l
  je m'appelle, ils s'appellent (but *vous vous appelez*)
- *envoyer* changes y to i
  j'envoie, ils envoient (but *nous envoyons*)

1 Underline the correct form of the verb.

a Je **rentre / rentres / rentrez** d'Écosse.

b Tu **préfère / préfères / préfèrent** porter un uniforme?!

c Mes parents **achète / achetons / achètent** des cadeaux en ligne.

d Elle **rêve / rêves / rêvent** d'habiter dans une grande maison.

e Vous **utilises / utilisons / utilisez** l'euro en Irlande?

f On **espère / espères / espèrent** voir le mont Blanc.

2 Underline the person (the subject pronoun) that matches each verb.

a Aujourd'hui, **tu / on / vous** organise une visite.

b Le soir, **je / tu / ils** joue aux jeux vidéo.

c **Je / Tu / Vous** déménages dans deux semaines?

d **Nous / Vous / Ils** payez les vêtements?

e **Fabien / Ils / Elles** partage une chambre.

f **Mon frère / Ma sœur / Mes parents** envoient un mail.

> **TIP**
>
> Even if you don't know
> some of the verbs on this
> page, they are all regular *-er*
> verbs, so you can work out
> the endings. Where there
> are slight changes, look for
> patterns and similarities to
> other verbs.

3 Write the correct form of each verb. Then draw lines to match the verbs to the English.

a Tu _____ ton travail à quelle heure? (*commencer*)

b Le problème, c'est que mes mails n' _____ pas. (*arriver*)

c Qu'est-ce que vous _____ faire? (*espérer*)

d Nous _____ dans un appartement. (*loger*)

e Ma chambre _____ ma personnalité. (*refléter*)

f J'_____ de limiter mon temps en ligne. (*essayer*)

1 to hope

2 to start

3 to try

4 to reflect

5 to arrive

6 to stay

Present tense of -ir verbs

1 **Circle the correct form of the verb, then match the sentences to the English.**

  a Nous **finis / finissons / finissez** le jeu après le dîner.

  b Mes grands-parents **choisis / choisit / choisissent** de voyager en car.

  c Mon chat **grossis / grossit / grossissent** parce qu'il est paresseux!

  d Julien et sa copine **rougis / rougit / rougissent** tout le temps.

  e Vous **réfléchis / réfléchissons / réfléchissez** trop longtemps.

  f Je **remplis / remplit / remplissez** le verre d'eau..

  1 You think for too long. ☐

  2 My cat is getting fat because he's lazy! ☐

  3 I'm filling the glass with water. ☐

  4 We're finishing the game after dinner. ☐

  5 Julien and his girlfriend blush all the time. ☐

  6 My grandparents choose to travel by coach. ☐

> Some regular verbs end in -ir in the infinitive.
> To form the present tense, take -ir off the infinitive (e.g. fin**ir** → fin-).
> Add the following endings:
>
> | je ___**is** | nous ___**issons** |
> | tu ___**is** | vous ___**issez** |
> | il/elle/on ___**it** | ils/elles ___**issent** |
>
> All the singular forms sound the same.
> You can apply this pattern to all regular -ir verbs, even if you have not met them before.

2 **Complete the crossword.**

Horizontalement

2 Il _____ puis il répond à la question. (9)

4 Léa et Alice sont malades, _____ vomissent! (5)

7 Nous _____ le voyage à Paris. (9)

8 Qu'est-ce que vous _____, le train ou le car? (10)

11 Ces garçons sont timides et _____ rougissent. (3)

12 Pour compléter les mots croisés, on _____ la grille. (7)

Verticalement

1 Quand mes copains travaillent, ils _____. (11)

3 Lola, _____ choisis le vélo ou le bus pour aller en ville? (2)

5 Mon hamster mange trop, il va _____! (7)

6 _____ réfléchissons parce que c'est une question difficile. (4)

9 Voilà Anna! _____ finit ses devoirs. (4)

10 Et Léon? _____ ne travaille pas, il réfléchit! (2)

> **TIP**
>
> Each answer is either a subject pronoun or a form of one of these verbs:
> choisir   finir   grossir
> réfléchir   remplir   réussir

Grammar

Present tense of –re verbs

> Some regular verbs end in *-re* in the infinitive.
> To form the present tense, take *-re* off the infinitive (e.g. *vend**re*** → *vend-*).
> Add the following endings:
>
> | | |
> |---|---|
> | je ____**s** | nous ____**ons** |
> | tu ____**s** | vous ____**ez** |
> | il/elle/on ____ | ils/elles ____**ent** |
>
> All the singular forms sound the same.
>
> Two common *-re* verbs are slightly irregular:
> * *mettre* (to put, put on) loses a 't' in the singular (*je mets, tu mets, il/elle met*)
> * *prendre* (to take) loses the 'd' in the plural (*nous pre**n**ons, vous pre**n**ez, ils/elles pre**nn**ent*)

1 Draw lines to match the sentence parts.

a Est-ce qu'il	**1** descendent du troisième étage.
b Quand le portable sonne, je ne	**2** met un pull.
c Est-ce que tu	**3** vend sa tablette?
d À la campagne, nous	**4** attendez devant le cinéma?
e Est-ce que vous	**5** réponds pas toujours.
f Mes parents	**6** entendons beaucoup d'animaux.
g Moi, je suis paresseuse, je	**7** perds des choses dans ta chambre?
h Quand il fait froid, on	**8** prends l'ascenseur.

2 Underline the correct part of the verb.

a Maintenant, nous **attends / attendons / attendez** le train.

b Mon copain ne **répond / réponds / répondez** jamais à mes textos.

c Moi, je **perds / perd / perdent** souvent mon portable. C'est embêtant!

d Pour aller au stade, vous **descendent / descendez / descend** la rue et c'est à gauche.

e Tu **entends / entend / entendez** la musique? Elle n'est pas très forte.

f Mes copains **vendons / vendez / vendent** des tickets pour le concert.

g Pour aller en ville, nous **prennent / prenez / prenons** le bus.

h Qu'est-ce que tu **mets / met / mettez** pour la fête?

3 Translate the sentences into French.

a I always reply to her texts. _____

b She never loses her phone. _____

c We're coming down the street now. _____

d What are we (*on*) wearing for the concert? _____

e My friends are waiting for the bus in town. _____

f Are you (*vous*) taking the lift? <u>I'm</u> going
down the stairs. _____

Present tense of regular verbs

In the present tense, **regular** verbs follow these patterns.

infinitive ends in:	-er	-ir	-re
je	__e	__is	__s
tu	__es	__is	__s
il/elle/on	__e	__it	__
nous	__ons	__issons	__ons
vous	__ez	__issez	__ez
ils/elles	__ent	__issent	__ent

Some verbs have slight differences in the stem (the main part), but the endings are the same. See pages 25 and 27 for some examples.

1 **Find the verbs in the word search. The first letter is given to start you off. Then write the infinitive and the English.**

je r__ __ __ __ __ __   *réussir*   *I succeed*

tu p__ __ __ __ __ __   _____ _____

il a__ __ __ __ __   _____ _____

elle c__ __ __ __ __ __   _____ _____

on t__ __ __ __ __ __ __   _____ _____

nous v__ __ __ __ __ __   _____ _____

vous f__ __ __ __ __ __ __   _____ _____

ils v__ __ __ __ __ __   _____ _____

elles r__ __ __ __ __ __ __   _____ _____

V	O	Y	A	G	E	N	T	I	L
E	A	T	R	B	C	D	R	E	P
N	A	R	É	G	H	I	A	J	R
D	T	L	U	N	O	P	V	R	É
O	T	S	S	U	I	V	A	Y	F
N	E	Z	S	H	S	J	I	L	È
S	N	N	I	P	I	R	L	S	R
S	D	O	S	R	T	V	L	R	E
E	F	I	N	I	S	S	E	Z	S
Z	R	É	P	O	N	D	E	N	T

Some verbs can add a prefix to create a new verb. For example, adding *re- (r-/ré-)* at the beginning is similar to the English re-
décorer (to decorate) – *redécorer* (to **re**decorate)
mettre (to put) – *remettre* (to put **back**)

These compound verbs follow exactly the same pattern as the verb they are formed from. The verb *com*prendre (to understand) is formed from *com-* + *prendre*, so it follows the same pattern as *prendre* (to take) – *nous prenons, nous* **com**prenons.

2 **Match the French to the English – write the correct number (1–6). Then fill the gap with the correct form of the verb.**

a ☐ Si tu ne _____ pas, il faut demander. (**comprendre**)

b ☐ Je _____ le paquet. (**renvoyer**)

c ☐ Il y a trop de devoirs – nous _____ ! (**désespérer**)

d ☐ Ils me _____ une grande fête. (**promettre**)

e ☐ Ah non! On _____ encore la même rue. (**redescendre**)

1 They are promising me a big party.

2 There's too much homework – we despair!

3 Oh no! We're going down the same street again.

4 I'm sending back the parcel.

5 If you don't understand, you must ask.

Grammar

Present tense of irregular verbs (1)

Some very common French verbs do not follow the regular patterns in the present tense and need to be learnt.
For *avoir* (to have) and *être* (to be), see pages 6–7.
For modal verbs (*devoir, pouvoir, vouloir*), see page 31.

	aller (to go)	faire (to do, make)	dire (to say)	*Many irregular verbs have these endings*
je	**vais**	**fais**	**dis**	...s
tu	**vas**	**fais**	**dis**	...s
il/elle/on	**va**	**fait**	**dit**	...t
nous	**allons**	**faisons**	**disons**	...ons
vous	**allez**	**faites**	**dites**	...ez
ils/elles	**vont**	**font**	**disent**	...ent

The verb *aller* is also used to form the near future tense (see page 33).

The verb *faire* can have different meanings in certain phrases (e.g. some weather expressions).

Here are some of the ways in which verbs are irregular:
- **écrire** (to write) adds 'v' in the plural (*nous écrivons, vous écrivez, ils/elles écrivent*).
- **boire** (to drink) adds 'v' in the plural and changes the vowel in the *nous/vous* forms (*nous buvons, vous buvez, ils/elles boivent*).
- **lire** (to read) adds 's' in the plural (*nous lisons, vous lisez, ils/elles lisent*).
  Others in this group are: *traduire* (to translate), *construire* (to build).

1 **Underline the irregular verbs and write the infinitives.**

  a Le week-end, je vais au centre sportif. (_____)

  b À la piscine, on fait de la natation. (_____)

  c On va au café. Tu bois de la limonade? (_____) (_____)

  d Mon copain et moi, nous buvons du thé. (_____)

  e Qu'est-ce que vous faites? (_____)

  f Nous traduisons une histoire en anglais. (_____)

  g Mes profs disent que j'écris très bien parce que je lis beaucoup de livres.
     (_____) (_____) (_____)

  h Nos voisins construisent une maison. Ils font beaucoup de bruit! (_____) (_____)

2 **Write the correct form of each verb.**

  a Qu'est-ce que tu _____ ? (**lire**)

  b Moi, j'_____ mon journal et mes sœurs _____ des mails. (**écrire** x 2)

  c En été, je _____ au bord de la mer. (**aller**)

  d Quand il _____ très chaud, nous ne _____ rien. (**faire** x 2)

  e Qu'est-ce que vous _____ ? (**dire**)

  f D'habitude, on _____ du coca. (**boire**)

3 **Write the English for the sentences in exercise 2.**

  a _____   d _____

  b _____   e _____

  c _____   f _____

Present tense of irregular verbs (2)

Most irregular verbs have these endings, but the stem usually changes:

je __s	nous __ons
tu __s	vous __ez
il/elle/on __t	ils/elles __ent

A number of irregular verbs have an infinitive ending in -oir.

	voir (to see)	recevoir (to receive, get)	savoir (to know (how))
je	vois	reçois	sais
tu	vois	reçois	sais
il/elle/on	voit	reçoit	sait
nous	voyons	recevons	savons
vous	voyez	recevez	savez
ils/elles	voient	reçoivent	savent

Some verbs fall into groups with similar patterns. Here are three groups.

	partir (to leave)	venir (to come)	ouvrir (to open)
je	pars	viens	ouvre
tu	pars	viens	ouvres
il/elle/on	part	vient	ouvre
nous	partons	venons	ouvrons
vous	partez	venez	ouvrez
ils/elles	partent	viennent	ouvrent
verbs with a similar pattern:	sortir (to go out) dormir (to sleep) (je dors, nous dormons)	devenir (to become) tenir (to hold) contenir (to contain)	couvrir (to cover) découvrir (to discover)

Note: *ouvrir* has the same endings as a regular **-er** verb.

1 Draw lines to match the sentence parts.

a Le samedi, je
b À quelle heure
c Mon cousin Tom
d Les scientifiques français
e Pourquoi est-ce que vous ne
f Avec nos lunettes nous
g Quand est-ce que vous
h S'il y a trop de bruit, je ne
i Qu'est ce qu'elle
j J'aime les magazines parce qu'ils

1 voyons mieux.
2 dors pas bien.
3 reçois 10€ de ma grand-mère.
4 contiennent des articles informatifs.
5 part le train?
6 sait dire en allemand?
7 découvrent beaucoup de choses.
8 ouvrez les portes?
9 vient du Québec.
10 sortez pas ce soir?

2 Complete the sentences with the correct form of the verbs.

a Est-ce que tu _____ ce soir? (**sortir**)
b Il _____ très riche, mais il ne _____ plus sa famille. (**devenir, voir**)
c On _____ en vacances en juillet. (**partir**)
d Nous _____ parler français! (**savoir**)
e Ils _____ de l'argent s'ils font des petits boulots. (**recevoir**)

3 Write a sentence of your choice in French for each verb.

a **partir** _____
b **sortir** _____
c **recevoir** _____

Modal verbs

The verbs *devoir* (to have to, must), *pouvoir* (to be able to, can) and *vouloir* (to want to) are irregular verbs known as modal verbs. They are usually followed by another verb in the infinitive.

devoir	pouvoir	vouloir
je dois	je peux	je veux
tu dois	tu peux	tu veux
il/elle/on doit	il/elle/on peut	il/elle/on veut
nous devons	nous pouvons	nous voulons
vous devez	vous pouvez	vous voulez
ils/elles doivent	ils/elles peuvent	ils/elles veulent
+ infinitive		

Je dois payer. (I must pay.)
Tu veux sortir. (Do you want to go out?)
On peut économiser. (We can save.)

Negative expressions go round the modal verb:
*Je **ne** peux **pas** sortir.* (I can't go out.)

In speech you can sometimes miss out the second verb.
On va au parc. Tu veux?
(We're going to the park. Do you want to come?)
Oui, je veux. / Non, je ne veux pas.
(Yes, I do. / No, I don't want to.)

1 **Complete the sentences with the correct form of *devoir, pouvoir* or *vouloir*.**

a Tu v_____ aller au concert?

b On d_____ économiser.

c Je p_____ gérer mon budget.

d Je ne d_____ pas payer mes sorties.

e On p_____ dépenser trop d'argent.

f Ils ne v_____ pas tondre la pelouse.

g Nous v_____ avoir beaucoup d'amis.

h Qu'est-ce que vous d_____ faire?

2 **Write a sentence for each picture, using the verb given in brackets.**

a Je _____ (devoir)

b Je ne _____ (devoir)

c Je _____ (pouvoir)

d _____ (pouvoir)

e _____ (vouloir)

a  b    c

d  e

> sortir avec mes copains   garder mon petit frère   jouer sur mon ordi le soir
> tondre la pelouse   économiser

3 **Write your own sentences in French, starting from the cues in English. Use the previous exercises and the suggestions in the box to help you.**

a (*I must*) _____

b (*I must not/I don't have to*) _____

c (*I can*) _____

d (*I can't*) _____

e (*I want to*) _____

f (*I don't want to*) _____

> faire du baby-sitting
> ranger ma chambre
> laver la voiture
> faire les courses
> aider à la maison
> faire mes devoirs
> rentrer tard le soir
> rentrer à l'heure

Grammar

Imperative

The imperative is used to give instructions or advice (e.g. discuss, do, talk).

Use the *tu* form of the present tense and leave out the word *tu*. For *-er* verbs you also miss off the final *s*.

tu parles → **parle** (talk)
tu finis → **finis** (finish)
tu attends → **attends** (wait)
tu fais → **fais** (do)

For an adult or more than one person, use the *vous* form of the present tense and leave out the word *vous*.

vous parlez → **parlez** (talk)
vous finissez → **finissez** (finish)
vous attendez → **attendez** (wait)
vous faites → **faites** (do)

In the negative, put *ne/n'* ... *pas* around the verb.
ne parle **pas** (don't talk)   **n'**attendez **pas** (don't wait)

Reflexive verbs (e.g. *se concentrer*) need *-toi* or *-vous* after the verb.
assieds-toi / asseyez-vous (sit down)
concentre-toi / concentrez-vous (concentrate)
But in the negative they have *te/t'* or *vous* before the verb.
ne t'assieds pas   *ne vous concentrez pas*

1 Draw lines to match the French to the English.

a Parle de tes problèmes.
b Fais tes devoirs tous les jours.
c Restez positifs.
d Demande à ton prof.
e Concentre-toi en classe.
f Ne dépense pas trop d'argent.
g Aidez vos parents à la maison.
h Ne reste pas dans ta chambre.
i Discutez de vos différences.
j Ne t'inquiète pas pour ton avenir.

1 Ask your teacher.
2 Don't spend too much money.
3 Do your homework every day.
4 Don't worry about your future.
5 Discuss your differences.
6 Talk about your problems.
7 Don't stay in your room.
8 Stay positive.
9 Concentrate in class.
10 Help your parents at home.

2 Which of those pieces of advice are directed at more than one person? Write the letters.

_____   _____   _____

3 Write the advice in French. Use the *tu* form.

a Discuss your problems.   _____
b Ask your parents.   _____
c Don't talk about your teacher!   _____
d Finish your homework in your room.   _____
e Help your friends.   _____

Near future tense

Use the present tense of *aller* (to go) with an infinitive to talk about what you are **going** to do in the near future.

je vais	nous allons	+ *infinitive*
tu vas	vous allez	*e.g.* acheter, regarder
il/elle/on va	ils/elles vont	

Je vais organiser *une fête.* **I'm going** to organise *a party.*

In the negative, put *ne ... pas, ne ... jamais* or *ne ... rien* around the part of *aller*.
Ce week-end, je **ne** *vais* **rien** *faire!* (This weekend, I'm not going to do anything!)
Vous **n'allez** **jamais** *être prêts!* (You're never going to be ready!)

1 **Complete the sentences using words from the box.**

> écouter   faire
> manger   nettoyer
> la salle   la vaisselle
> de la musique   de la pizza

a  **b**

c  **d**

a On va _____

b Ils vont _____

c Je ne vais pas _____

d Vous allez _____

2 **Complete the sentences with the correct form of *aller*.**

a Nous _____ organiser une fête.

b Laura, tu _____ envoyer les invitations?

c Je _____ aller au supermarché pour les boissons.

d Lucile et Samira _____ acheter la nourriture.

e On ne _____ pas manger trop de chips?

f Julien _____ télécharger de la musique.

g Sacha et Hugo, qu'est-ce que vous _____ faire?

h Ils ne _____ pas décorer la salle.

3 **Write four sentences of your choice using the near future tense. Use a negative in at least one of the sentences (*ne ... pas, ne ... jamais, ne ... rien*).**

_____

_____

_____

_____

Future tense

▶ *Allez 2 Student Book* **5.4, 5.5, 5.6**

To say what you **will do** (in the future), use the future tense.
For most verbs, add the future endings to the infinitive (but leave out the final *e* of *-re* verbs).

infinitive		stem	endings	meaning
jouer	je		**ai**	*I will play*
(*to play*)	tu	**jouer-**	**as**	*you will play*
choisir	il/elle/on		**a**	*he/she/we will choose*
(*to choose*)	nous	**choisir-**	**ons**	*we will choose*
boire	vous		**ez**	*you will drink*
(*to drink*)	ils/elles	**boir-**	**ont**	*they will drink*

Tip: if you know the present tense of *avoir* (see page 6), you have most of the endings for the future tense.

Watch out for *acheter* – it adds a grave accent (as it does in parts of the present tense): *j'achèterai* (I will buy)

1   Underline the future tense verbs, then draw lines to match the French to the English.

a   Je mangerai des légumes à chaque repas.

b   Sa vie ne changera pas beaucoup.

c   Tu réussiras à trouver un bon emploi.

d   Elles dormiront huit heures par nuit.

e   On attendra devant la piscine.

f   Est-ce que vous prendrez le train?

1   His life will not change much.

2   Will you take the train?

3   They will sleep for eight hours a night.

4   I'll eat vegetables at every meal.

5   You will succeed in finding a good job.

6   We'll wait outside the pool.

2   Complete the sentences with the correct form of the future tense. Say what they mean in English.

a   Nous _____ moins de fast-food. (**manger**)

b   Il ne _____ pas de boissons sucrées. (**boire**)

c   Ils _____ une grande maison. (**acheter**)

d   Quand est-ce que vous _____ en vacances? (**partir**)

e   Je ne _____ pas dans un bureau. (**travailler**)

f   J'espère que tu _____ à mes mails. (**répondre**)

3   Complete the sentences with a verb from the box, then say what each sentence means in English.

enverrai   ferons   ira   serez   verras   viendront

a   L'année prochaine, nous _____ plus de sport.

b   Mon prof _____ au collège à vélo.

c   Mes grands-parents _____ au restaurant.

d   Tu _____ tes cousins pour la première fois.

e   Dans dix ans, vous _____ très riches!

f   Je _____ un mail tous les jours.

Some verbs are irregular in the future tense, but it is just the **stem** that is irregular – the **endings are the same** for all verbs. Here are some common irregular verbs:

infinitive	stem
avoir (*to have*)	aur-
être (*to be*)	ser-
aller (*to go*)	ir-
faire (*to do*)	fer-
venir (*to come*)	viendr-
voir (*to see*)	verr-
envoyer (*to send*)	enverr-
pouvoir (*to be able*)	pourr-

To say what you **did** or **have done** in the past, use the perfect tense. It has two parts:

auxiliary = present tense of *avoir*	+ past participle		example and meaning
j'**ai** tu **as**	-*er* verbs: take -*er* off the infinitive and add **-é**	jou**er** → jou- → jou**é**	j'ai joué *(I played / I have played)*
il/elle/on **a** nous **avons**	-*ir* verbs: take -*ir* off the infinitive and add **-i**	fin**ir** → fin- → fin**i**	elle a fini *(she finished / she has finished)*
vous **avez** ils/elles **ont**	-*re* verbs: take -*re* off the infinitive and add **-u**	vend**re** → vend- → vend**u**	ils ont vendu *(they sold / they have sold)*

Negative expressions go around the auxiliary (*avoir*):
*Hier, il **n'**a **pas** joué au tennis.* (Yesterday he didn't play tennis.)
*Nous **n'**avons **rien** vendu.* (We didn't sell anything.)

1 **Circle the correct form of *avoir*.**

a Je n'(**ai**)/ **as** / **a** pas entendu le prof.

b Olivier **ai** / **as** /(**a**)vendu son ordinateur.

c Est-ce que tu **ai** /(**as**)/ **a** fini ton livre?

d Mes copains **a** / **avez** /(**ont**)mangé tous les biscuits.

e Hier soir, nous **a** /(**avons**)/ **ont** joué au volley.

f Vous **avons** (**avez**)/ **ont** réussi à boire deux litres de coca!

2 **Complete each sentence with the past participle of the verb.**

a J'ai ___attendu___ longtemps. (**attendre**)

b Tu as ___choisi___ un cadeau? (**choisir**)

c Nous avons ___écouté___ de la musique. (**écouter**)

d Pasteur a ___inventé___ un vaccin contre la rage. (**inventer**)

e Vous avez ___perdu___ quelque chose? (**perdre**)

f Ils ont ___préparé___ un grand repas. (**préparer**)

g Elle n'a pas ___rempli___ la bouteille. (**remplir**)

h Tu n'as pas ___répondu___ à mon message. (**répondre**)

3 **Translate the sentences into French. Use exercises 1 and 2 and the words in the box to help you.**

a Did you wait for the teacher? ___Tu as attendu pour le professor.___

b They have lost a bottle of cola. ___Ils ont perdu une bouteille de cola.___

c We have chosen some music for the party.
___Nous avons choisi la musique pour la fête.___

d Lucie loved the meal – she found the dessert delicious.
___Elle (Lucie) a adoré le menu – elle a trouvé le dessert délicieux___

e I slept for a long time – I didn't hear anything.
___J'ai dormi___

f He didn't think and he sent a photo online.
___Il ne réfléchi pas, et il a envoyé un photo en ligne___

adorer
envoyer
trouver
dormir
réfléchir
bien
le dessert
la fête
délicieux
en ligne

Perfect tense with avoir (2) ▶ *Allez 2 Student Book 1.6, 5.6*

The perfect tense has two parts: the **auxiliary** (usually part of *avoir*) and the **past participle**. Some past participles are irregular; here are some common ones. It might help you to learn them in groups, as set out here.

faire – *j'ai* **fait** (I did/have done)
écrire – *j'ai* **écrit** (I wrote/have written)
dire – *j'ai* **dit** (I said/have said)

construire – *j'ai* **construit** (I built/have built)
mettre – *j'ai* **mis** (I put/have put)
prendre – *j'ai* **pris** (I took/have taken)

ouvrir – *j'ai* **ouvert** (I opened/have opened)

avoir – *j'ai* **eu** (I had/have had)
voir – *j'ai* **vu** (I saw/have seen)
boire – *j'ai* **bu** (I drank/have drunk)
lire – *j'ai* **lu** (I read/have read)
pouvoir – *j'ai* **pu** (I have been able to/could)
devoir – *j'ai* **dû** (I have had to)
vouloir – *j'ai* **voulu** (I wanted to)

Compounds of these verbs follow the same pattern.
prendre – *j'ai* **pris**; *comprendre* – *j'ai com***pris**
(I have understood)

Negative expressions go round the auxiliary.
Il **n'a pas** *voulu partir.* (He didn't want to leave.)

1 Underline the past participles, then draw lines to match the French to the English.

a Ils ont <u>eu</u> des problèmes.
b Un Belge a <u>écrit</u> la BD *Tintin*.
c On a <u>dû</u> nettoyer la salle.
d Il a <u>pu</u> changer la date de la fête.
e J'ai déjà <u>lu</u> ce livre.*
f Elle n'a rien <u>bu</u> de toute la journée.

1 I have already read this book.
2 They've had some problems.
3 She didn't drink anything all day.
4 A Belgian wrote the *Tintin* comic books.
5 He's been able to change the date of the party.
6 We had to clean the room.

*déjà (already) goes between the auxiliary and the past participle.

2 Complete the sentences with the perfect tense of the irregular verbs. Remember that you need <u>two</u> words each time. Then write the English meaning.

a Il __a bu__ du coca. (**boire**) — he drank the coke.
b Qu'est-ce que tu __as dit__ ? (**dire**) — what did you say ?
c Je n'__ai__ rien __fait__ . (**faire**) — I haven't done anything.
d Nous __avons lu__ des BD. (**lire**) — we have read the comic
e Ils __ont ouvert__ les portes. (**ouvrir**) — They have opened the doors
f Elle n'__a__ pas __pris__ le train. (**prendre**) — she hasn't taken the train

3 Complete the sentences with the perfect tense of the verbs. Watch out – some are regular, some irregular.

a Ma copine __a acheté__ une nouvelle robe. (**acheter**)
b Je n'__ai__ pas __comprendu__ la question. (**comprendre**)
c Gustave Eiffel __a construit__ une tour à Paris. (**construire**)
d Tu __as ecrir__ des mails? (**écrire**)
e Vous _____ beaucoup d'argent? (**gagner**)
f Elles n'__ont mangé__ de salade. (**manger**)
g Nous __avons mis__ un pull. (**mettre**)
h Qu'est-ce qu'ils _____ au zoo? (**voir**)

Grammar

Perfect tense with être

A few verbs form the perfect tense with **être** instead of **avoir** as the auxiliary. These are usually verbs involving movement from one place to another.

If the subject (*je, tu* etc.) is feminine, you need to add an extra **-e** to the past participle.

If the subject is plural, add **-s**. If it is feminine **and** plural, add **-es**.

Here is the perfect tense of **aller** (to go):

je suis	allé/allé**e**	nous sommes	allé**s**/allé**es**
tu es	allé/allé**e**	vous êtes	allé/allé**e**/ allé**s**/allé**es**
il est	allé	ils sont	allé**s**
elle est	allé**e**	elles sont	allé**es**
on est	allé**s**/allé**es**		

Here are the verbs that follow this pattern – it might help you to learn them in twos and threes:

venir – je suis venu(e) (I came)
aller – je suis allé(e) (I went)
　　entrer – je suis entré(e) (I came in)
　　sortir – je suis sorti(e) (I went out)
　　retourner – je suis retourné(e) (I returned)
arriver – je suis arrivé(e) (I arrived)
partir – je suis parti(e) (I left)
　　monter – je suis monté(e) (I went up)
　　descendre – je suis descendu(e) (I went down)
rester – je suis resté(e) (I stayed)
tomber – je suis tombé(e) (I fell)
　　naître – je suis né(e) (I was born)
　　mourir – il (elle) est mort(e) (he/she died)

Compounds of these verbs also follow the pattern:
rentrer *– je suis* **rentré***(e)* (I came home)
re*venir – Je suis* **re***venu(e)* (I came back)
de*venir – je suis* **de***venu(e)* (I became)

1 Complete the sentences with the correct part of *être*.

a Je _____ arrivée à midi.

b Nous _____ partis hier.

c Mes parents _____ nés en Suisse.

d Tu _____ sorti hier soir, Luc?

e Mon père _____ rentré samedi.

f Vous _____ restées à la maison?

2 Underline the correct past participle in each sentence.

a Annie, tu es **allé** / **allée** / **allées** au festival?

b Oui, je suis **partie** / **partis** / **parties** avec Lucie.

c Mes copains ne sont pas **venu** / **venue** / **venus**.

d Adam, tu es **né** / **née** / **nées** en avril?

e Ma tante est **devenu** / **devenue** / **devenues** très riche.

f Nous sommes **monté** / **montée** / **montés** dans le bus.

3 Answer the questions in French using *être* verbs. Use the suggestions in the box if you want.

a Tu es né(e) quand?

　　Je _____

b Qu'est-ce que tu as fait samedi?

　　Je _____

c Qu'est-ce que vous avez fait cet été?

　　Nous _____

> aller au bord de la mer
> monter au premier
> 　　étage de la tour Eiffel
> partir en vacances
> rester à la maison
> tomber de mon vélo/
> 　　skateboard/cheval
> le 10 novembre/avril/…
> en octobre/mai/…

Perfect tense with avoir and être

▶ *Allez 2 Student Book*
1.6, 6.6

- Use the perfect tense to say what you **did** or **have done** in the past.
- Most verbs use *avoir* as the auxiliary (see pages 35–36).
- A few verbs use *être* as the auxiliary – they mostly involve movement from one place to another (see page 37).
- Regular past participles end in **-é**, **-i** or **-u** (see page 35).
- Some past participles are irregular (see pages 36–37).
- The past participle of *être* verbs needs to agree with the subject (see page 37).

1 Complete the table.

infinitive	meaning to ...	past participle	avoir/ être
attendre	wait (for)	attendu	avoir
boire			
choisir			
descendre			être
faire			
finir			
manger			
monter			

infinitive	meaning to ...	past participle	avoir/ être
naître			
partir			
payer			
perdre			
regarder			
sortir			
tomber			
venir			

2 Complete Alice's blog with the correct part of *avoir* or *être*.

Le week-end dernier, je **(a)** _____ allée à un festival avec mon frère Nico et sa copine Léa. Nous **(b)** _____ partis à 10 heures et nous **(c)** _____ pris le train et le bus. On **(d)** _____ arrivés à midi et heureusement, il **(e)** _____ fait soleil. J' **(f)** _____ écouté beaucoup de musique – tous les groupes **(g)** _____ bien joué et on **(h)** _____ pu danser pendant tout le festival. Ce que je n' **(i)** _____ pas aimé, c'est qu'on **(j)** _____ attendu longtemps pour aller aux toilettes! Le soir, Léa et Nico **(k)** _____ mangé un hamburger mais moi, j' **(l)** _____ préféré manger des crêpes. À 23 heures ma mère **(m)** _____ venue me chercher. Nico et Léa **(n)** _____ restés au festival. Maman et moi, nous **(o)** _____ arrivées très tard chez nous et j' **(p)** _____ dormi jusqu'à midi!

3 Write a few sentences about where you went and what you did recently. This doesn't have to be true – but it does have to be in the perfect tense! Try to use verbs with *avoir* and *être*, both regular and irregular. Use exercises 1 and 2 to help you.

_____

_____

_____

_____

Grammar

Imperfect tense

The imperfect tense is used to talk about what **used to happen** or what **was happening** in the past.

To form the imperfect:
- take the *nous* form of the present tense (e.g. *jouons/finissons*)
- take off the *-ons* ending (e.g. *jou-/finiss-*)
- add these endings:

je	__**ais**	nous	__**ions**
tu	__**ais**	vous	__**iez**
il/elle/on	__**ait**	ils/elles	__**aient**

*On **jouait** dans la rue.* We used to play in the street.
*Je **finissais** mes devoirs à 20 heures.* I used to finish my homework at 8pm.

Use the imperfect of *être* to describe what someone or something was like. It is the only verb with an irregular stem (**ét-**), but the endings are the same as other verbs. The most common use of this form is **c'était** (it was) with an adjective, e.g. *c'était génial.*

1 Match the pictures to the captions (write the number). Then underline the imperfect tense verbs.

Quand j'étais jeune …

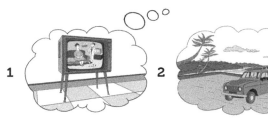  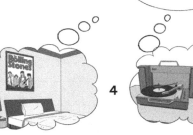 

1 2 3 4

a `3` J'étais fan des Rolling Stones. Il y avait un poster sur le mur de ma chambre.
b `4` Le soir, mes amis et moi, nous écoutions des disques.
c `1` Les émissions à la télé étaient en noir et blanc. On n'avait pas la télé en couleur.
d `2` Mon père avait une Renault 4, elle était super! On allait souvent à la mer.

2 Complete the sentences with the correct form of the imperfect tense.

a Quand j'___*ai*___ (**avoir**) six ans, je ___*joue*___ (**jouer**) souvent avec mes poupées.

b À l'âge de quatre ans, je ne ___*choisis*___ (**choisir**) pas mes vêtements.

c À l'école primaire, c'___*es*___ (**être**) super. Nous ___*avons*___ (**avoir**) un lapin dans la salle de classe.

d J'___*habite*___ (**habiter**) à la campagne. Pour aller à l'école, on _____ (**attendre**) le bus devant la maison.

e Quand j'___*etait*___ (**être**) jeune, je ne ___*pouvais*___ (**pouvoir**) pas regarder la télé le soir.

f Mes parents _____ (**être**) assez stricts.

une poupée

un lapin

3 Write three sentences about what life used to be like when you were younger.

_____

_____

_____

Depuis means 'since' or 'for'. In English it is used with the past tense ('<u>have</u> done'), but in French it is used with the <u>present tense</u> (because you are still doing whatever it is).

Je connais Max **depuis** *trois ans.* (<u>I have known</u> Max **for** three years. ... and I still know him)
J'y habite **depuis** *l'âge de cinq ans.* (<u>I have lived</u> here **since** I was five. ... and I still live here)

1 **Draw lines to join the sentence parts.**

a Je joue dans un club de
b Mes parents vendent
c Ils travaillent dans la
d Nous habitons sur un
e Depuis deux semaines,
f Ma copine est malade

1 il y a des problèmes au centre-ville.
2 foot depuis trois ans.
3 bateau depuis le mois de juin.
4 des voitures depuis vingt ans.
5 depuis hier soir.
6 banlieue de Dijon depuis cinq ans.

2 **Translate the completed sentences from exercise 1 into English.**

a _____
b _____
c _____
d _____
e _____
f _____

3 **Answer the questions in French.**

a Tu habites où et depuis combien de temps?

_____

b Tu apprends le français depuis quand?

_____

c Tu connais ton meilleur ami / ta meilleure amie depuis combien de temps?

_____

4 **Translate these sentences into English.**

a Elle attendait depuis trente minutes quand le bus est arrivé.

_____

b Tu travaillais depuis combien de temps quand j'ai téléphoné?

_____

c Je jouais en ligne depuis trois heures quand mon père m'a demandé d'arrêter!

_____

You can also use *depuis* with the <u>imperfect tense</u> to say what you <u>had been doing</u> further back in the past.
J'y <u>habitais</u> depuis trois ans quand mon frère est arrivé.
(I <u>had been living</u> there for three years when my brother arrived.)

quand and si

Quand (when) is a question word, but it can also be used to join sentences together. Here are examples, used with present and imperfect tense verbs, similar to English.
*Quand il **fait** beau, je **joue** au tennis.* (When it **is** fine, I **play** tennis.)
*Quand j'**étais** jeune, je **voulais** être médecin.* (When I **was** young, I **wanted** to be a doctor.)

Quand is used differently from English when talking about the future.
*Quand j'**aurai** 30 ans, je **serai** célèbre.* (When I **am** 30, I **will be** famous.)
English uses the present tense (when I **am** 30), but French is more logical and uses the future tense: the speaker is not yet 30, so says that when they **will be** 30, in the future, they will be famous.

1 Draw lines to match the French to the English.

a Quand il pleut, je ne sors pas.

b Quand j'avais quatre ans, je jouais avec mon éléphant en peluche.

c Quand ma grand-mère était jeune, l'euro n'existait pas.

d Quand j'irai au cinéma, je regarderai un film comique.

e Quand j'aurai 16 ans, je pourrai faire un petit boulot.

1 When I go to the cinema, I will watch a comedy.

2 When it is raining, I don't go out.

3 When I am 16, I will be able to have a job.

4 When I was four, I played with my toy elephant.

5 When my grandma was young, the euro didn't exist.

2 Look again at the French sentences in exercise 1. Underline the present tense verbs, circle the imperfect tense verbs and highlight the future tense verbs.

3 Complete the sentences using phrases from the box.

a Quand je n'ai pas de devoirs, _____

b Quand j'avais six ans, _____

c Quand j'aurai 18 ans, _____

> je voulais être pilote.
> je partirai en vacances
> avec mes copains.
> je suis très content.

Use *si* (if) with the present tense, followed by a clause in the future tense, in a similar way to English.
*Si je **peux**, j'**irai** au concert.* (If I **can**, I **will go** to the concert.)

Si is only shortened to *s'* before *il* and *ils* (and not before *elle, elles* and *on*).
*S'il **fait** beau, je **jouerai** au tennis.* (If it **is** fine, I **will play** tennis.)
*Si elle **joue** bien, je ne **gagnerai** pas.* (If she **plays** well, I **will** not **win.**)

4 Complete the sentences with the appropriate future tense verb.

a Si j'ai le temps, je _____ le musée.

b Si on peut, on _____ au supermarché.

c S'il fait mauvais, je _____ chez moi.

d Si on peut, on _____ du camping.

> fera
> resterai
> travaillera
> visiterai

Conditional

▶ *Allez 2 Student Book*
8.4, 8.6, 9.3, 9.6

To say what you **would do**, use the **conditional**.
To form the conditional of regular verbs:
• take the infinitive, e.g. *jouer, finir, vendre* (but leave out the final *e* of *-re* verbs)
• add these endings – exactly the same as in the **imperfect** tense (see page 39):

je __**ais**		*nous* __**ions**	
tu __**ais**		*vous* __**iez**	
il/elle/on __**ait**	*ils/elles* __**aient**		

je **jouer**ais (I would play)
tu **finir**ais (you would finish)
il **vendr**ait (he would sell)

The endings are the same for all verbs, but some verbs have an irregular **stem**.
This stem is exactly the same as in the **future** tense (see page 34).

infinitive	stem	conditional	meaning
avoir (*to have*)	aur-	j'**aur**ais	*I would have*
être (*to be*)	ser-	tu **ser**ais	*you would be*
aller (*to go*)	ir-	il **ir**ait	*he would go*
faire (*to do*)	fer-	elle **fer**ait	*she would do*
venir (*to come*)	viendr-	nous **viendr**ions	*we would come*
voir (*to see*)	verr-	vous **verr**iez	*you would see*
envoyer (*to send*)	enverr-	ils **enverr**aient	*they would send*
pouvoir (*to be able*)	pourr-	elles **pourr**aient	*they would be able*
vouloir (*to want*)	voudr-	je **voudr**ais	*I would like*

Elle **serait** *très riche, si …* (She would be very rich if …)
Je **voudrais** *aller au cinéma.* (I'd like to go to the cinema.)

1 Draw lines to match the sentence parts, then give the English for them.

a Je voudrais habiter dans
b La maison de mes rêves
c Moi, j'achèterais un bel
d Mes amis me
e Mes parents aimeraient
f Feriez-vous construire
g Oui, elle aurait toutes les
h Et toi, qu'est-ce que

1 faire le tour du monde.
2 nouvelles technologies.
3 une ferme à la campagne.
4 appartement au centre de Paris.
5 tu ferais?
6 serait une villa au bord de la mer.
7 une maison écologique?
8 rendraient souvent visite.

> Use *si* (if) with the <u>imperfect</u> tense, together with a verb in the **conditional**.
> *Si je <u>gagnais</u> à la loterie, j'*irais *en vacances.* (If I <u>won</u> the lottery, I **would go** on holiday.)
> *Si j'<u>étais</u> riche, je ne* **travaillerais** *pas.* (If I <u>were</u> rich, I **would** not **work**.)

2 Complete the sentences as you wish, using the conditional.
Use exercise 1 and the words in the box to help you.

a Si je gagnais à la loterie, _____

b Si j'étais très riche, _____

c Si je pouvais être un super-héros/une super-héroïne, _____
_____

> aider les pauvres   donner
> choisir   me rendre invisible
> sauver l'univers   voler

Grammar

Using several tenses together

It is important to recognise and use different tenses in French.
You have met the infinitive, four different tenses and the conditional.
* **infinitive** – the basic form of the verb – 'to ...' (*jouer, descendre*)
* **present** – what happens regularly or is happening now (*je joue, je descends*)
* **perfect** – what happened or has happened in the past (*j'ai joué, je suis descendu(e)*)
* **imperfect** – describing what used to happen or was happening in the past (*je jouais, je descendais*)
* **future** – what will happen in the future – often used with *quand* (when) (*je jouerai, je descendrai*); sometimes replaced by *aller* + infinitive – what is going to happen in the **near future** (*je vais jouer, je vais descendre*)
* **conditional** – what would happen – often used with *si* (if) + imperfect (*je jouerais, je descendrais*)

Look back at the Workbook pages that practise the different tenses. Familiarise yourself with the way they are formed, their endings, the exceptions (irregular verbs) and the way they are used.

1 Fill in the missing forms of the verbs.

infinitive	present	perfect	imperfect	future	conditional
travailler	je _____	j'ai travaillé	je _____	je _____	je travaillerais
choisir	tu choisis	tu _____	tu _____	tu choisiras	tu _____
vendre	il _____	il _____	il vendait	il vendra	il _____
avoir	elle a	elle a eu	elle _____	elle _____	elle aurait
être	on est	on a été	on _____	on sera	on _____
faire	nous faisons	nous _____	nous faisions	nous _____	nous ferions
aller	vous _____	vous êtes allé(e)s	vous _____	vous irez	vous _____
pouvoir	ils peuvent	ils ont pu	ils _____	ils _____	ils pourraient

2 Complete the conversation with the correct verb from the box.

– La vie **(a)** _____ différente quand tu **(b)** _____ jeune?

– Oui, je n' **(c)** _____ pas de téléphone portable et on **(d)** _____ la musique sur un tourne-disque.

– Qu'est-ce que tu **(e)** _____ comme métier?

– J' **(f)** _____ dans une banque et après ça, j' **(g)** _____ des voitures.

– Moi, j' **(h)** _____ le théâtre et je **(i)** _____ être actrice. Je **(j)** _____ mes études et quand j' **(k)** _____ 25 ans, je **(l)** _____ riche et célèbre!

adore	ai travaillé	ai vendu
as fait	aurai	avais
écoutait	étais	était
finirai	serai	voudrais

3 Write something about yourself, using at least three different tenses.

_____

_____

_____

Unit 1: Cultural awareness strategies

You have no doubt noticed similarities and differences between French-speaking and English-speaking cultures. As you work through *Allez 2*, question things! Studying History and Geography alongside a foreign language is very useful, but why? You learn a great deal about how a country is today from its past. Doing Internet research for Geography (and other subjects), shows images from across the world that reveal more than just the local weather conditions. How carefully do you look? Are you really observant? Do you question why things are different? Think about how this can help you understand the language, the people and life in French-speaking countries better.

1 **Pair work. List as many differences and similarities as you can between France and the UK. Don't look anything up! Use *on* in your statements.**

a Similarities

Example: On joue au tennis. Il y a un grand tournoi de tennis.

_____

_____

_____

b Differences

Example: On utilise l'euro en France et la livre sterling en Grande-Bretagne.

_____

_____

_____

2 **Why do people sometimes move to a new country? Think of any famous people, such as footballers and musicians, who have moved to the UK from another country. Write their names and where they moved from. What do you think they might have found strange here? (Write notes in English.)**

_____

_____

3 **In Unit 8 you will find out about the life-changing influence of a new country on artists like Van Gogh (Dutch) and Cézanne (French). Research the life of the French artist Paul Gauguin and write some facts about him, particularly where he travelled and what influence this had on his painting.**

Suggested websites: *www.impressionniste.net/gauguin.htm*
www.musee-orsay.fr   *www.bbc.co.uk/arts/yourpaintings/artists/paul-gauguin*

_____

_____

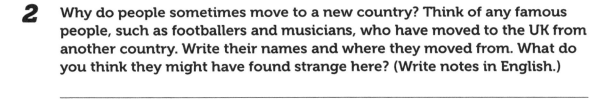

French is a world language, spoken around the globe, so it is well worth motivating yourself to learn to speak it well! Are you still using strategies that you found worked for you last year, such as colour-coding masculine and feminine nouns or recording new vocabulary on your phone to listen to it often?

Three top tips:

1 Plan how to go about learning something by heart – this is the key to success!

2 Once you have decided what you want to learn, set yourself time targets: you could test yourself the next day and then again a week later.

3 Try a new strategy, like using dice games or acronyms (see page 15, Student Book).

1 **Try to memorise these facts about France, using the strategies above and on page 15 of the Student Book. Tick the box on the right when you have learnt them and can say them from memory in French one week later with good pronunciation. Be motivated and really determined!**

a La France: on l'appelle l'Hexagone à cause de sa forme. ☐

b La France est deux fois plus grande que la Grande-Bretagne. ☐

c En Europe, à part la France, les francophones se trouvent en Belgique (45% de la population), en Suisse (20%) et au Luxembourg (14%). ☐

2 **As you know, many countries in Africa have French, not English, as one of their official languages. Unjumble these names of countries from the French-speaking world – _la francophonie_.**

a ligeérA _____

b elI euraciM _____

c ieryS _____

d coMra _____

3 **Separate the words with correct punctuation to make four sentences about _la francophonie_. Write the sentences out correctly.**

Onparlefrançaisdansunpaysfrancophoneilyaplusde150millionsdefrancophones danslemondeilshabitentdansplusdequarantepayssurlescinqcontinentsle françaisestunelanguetrèstrèsimportantecar...

_____

_____

_____

_____

An additional challenge! Add a phrase to complete the fourth sentence, to say why it is important to learn French. When your teacher has checked your answer, record your statement on your phone and learn it by heart.

When you see a longer reading text, don't panic! Break it down with your strategies.
- Use what you know about your own language to help you to pick out **cognates**.
- Use strategies you have learnt, like **contextualising**, to work out unknown words.
- Find **opinions** – are there clues about whether the opinion is positive or negative?
- Look out for **punctuation**, as it can give a clue to the meaning.

La Polynésie française

La France a conservé quelques territoires dispersés aux quatre coins du globe.Les touristes adorent la Polynésie française, située en plein cœur de l'océan Pacifique, car c'est l'été toute l'année! De mars à novembre, c'est la saison sèche avec des températures de 22 à 27°C. De décembre à février, c'est la saison humide avec des températures de 25 à 35°C.

La Polynésie française est un espace maritime de 4 millions de km² avec 118 îles, une surface équivalente à celle de l'Europe. On peut y observer des baleines et des dauphins! On peut admirer les danses tahitiennes et faire des activités aquatiques comme la plongée sous-marine. Il y a aussi beaucoup de sites de surf.

1 The text above is from a tourist brochure about the islands of French Polynesia. Skim through it and tick the topics that are mentioned:

a temperature ☐ **b** total area ☐ **c** wildlife ☐ **d** activities ☐

2 Read it more closely and find five cognates. *Example: globe*

_____

3 Find in the extract five words you have never seen before. Use a dictionary to find their meanings. If they are nouns, note their gender, M or F. Then record them in your vocabulary book or on your phone. *Example: coin (M) = corner*

4 Read another extract from the brochure, about a famous visitor to Tahiti. See if you can pick out the answers to the questions.

a When did Gauguin visit Van Gogh?_____ **b** How old was he then?_____

c Where is Arles? _____

d In Tahiti, what is especially good for artists? (3 things) _____

_____

Paul Gauguin

Le peintre Paul Gauguin est né en France en 1848. Il a rendu visite à Van Gogh en 1888 à Arles, dans le sud de la France. En 1891, Gauguin a voyagé dans les îles polynésiennes, à Tahiti, où les plages, les fleurs et les couleurs sont magnifiques pour les peintres.

Time for **thinking** and **planning** before you start writing any French is very useful. In Allez 2 Unit 2 you read film and book reviews and took on the role of a music journalist (page 25 of the Student Book). You were asked to describe films and books that you have strong opinions about, and to use **spidergrams** to help you plan (page 27).

Spend two minutes reflecting on the strategy of using bubbles in spidergrams (or boxes in mind maps if you prefer). Do you find this a logical process? Write down a few thoughts in English about this way of working, both in French lessons and in other subjects where you write essays. Take this seriously: it will help improve your study habits, particularly drafting and re-drafting.

1 Make your spidergram, using the reminder on the right.

2 Draw a scene from the film or book, or print a picture you find online. This will give you more ideas of things to say, as well as making the finished review more interesting.

3 Find some more adjectives and phrases to describe the people or place in your picture.

4 Show your spidergram notes and picture to your partner or your teacher. Is it useful to get feedback at this stage or after the first draft of writing? What do you find most helpful, and why?

5 Pair work. Which words and phrases in your notes are more difficult to write accurately? Highlight three items in your notes and ask a partner to dictate them to you. Write them out and check the spelling in a dictionary.

6 Write the whole review. Add some more advanced structures, using the key language boxes in Unit 2 (see page 31 of the Student Book). To give your overall judgement, think about your answer to these two questions:

Spidergrams: a reminder
Centre bubble   Title of the film or book
Bubble 1   List the key facts: where, when, who
Bubble 2   Use language that you know already to give some details about the characters
Bubble 3   Add key words to give opinions (and reasons why)
Bubble 4   Say who you think this film/book would be suitable for

Work through activities 1–6 to write the best review you can. First choose your film or book.

Combien d'étoiles (sur 5) donnerais-tu à ce film/livre?

Est-ce que tu recommanderais ce film/livre? Pourquoi (pas)?

Unit 3: Memorisation strategies

Memorising the long words in this unit can be tricky, so first recap the strategies from *Allez 1*. Here are some new strategies to try:
- Break the words up and try to spot familiar **prefixes** and **suffixes**, as in these examples: *démodé*, *télécharger*, *absolument*.
- Use an online **word cloud** creator such as *Wordle* or *WordItOut*. Print out your word cloud to stick on the wall, so that you can see the vocabulary you need to memorise in a different way.
- **Label** items in your bedroom and around the house with sticky notes so that you see them often.
- Close your eyes and try to **visualise** the words you want to learn.

1 The list on the right gives some of the trickier words from Unit 3.

   a Set a timer for three minutes and look at the words very carefully.

   b Now close your eyes and try to see them in your head. In your mind, try to relate them to your life.

   c Set the timer for one minute, cover the words up and write them from memory. Then check them and check your spelling.

fiable
divertissant
la vie virtuelle
premièrement
un écran tactile
la cybersécurité
des réseaux sociaux
les nouvelles technologies

2 Pair work. Find in Unit 3 five more words or phrases each that you need to learn. Read them aloud, so that you hear all ten words twice. Try to memorise them and then set yourselves a test, devising your own mark scheme. Mark each other's answers.

3 Try combining two strategies: creating a word cloud and using word categories. Look at the lists on page 57 of the Student Book. Write as many words as you can into a table like the one below, sorting them into nouns, adjectives, verbs.

Then make a word cloud online for each column of the table. Customise them with fonts and colours that appeal to you. Print them out, put them on your wall or share your best one with your friends online.

nouns	adjectives	verbs
écran tactile	nouvelle	présentent
applis	nouveau	se protéger
sites	léger	

Skills

> Strategies you know already and can build on:
> - **Before** you start speaking, plan what you want to say.
> - Say any long or tricky words **aloud** to practise them. Watch out for the accents!
> - **Recycle** familiar set phrases from other themes you have already covered. For example, use hesitation strategies – they give you time to think.
>
> New strategies to try:
> - Use an **all-purpose** word like *le truc* if you get stuck or forget the name of something.
> - Use a word with **roughly the same** meaning. If you forget the word for a laptop, for example, say *petit ordinateur*.

1 **Pair work. Practise saying these words and phrases out loud with the best French accent possible! Say them several times over and try to sound French.**

   a iPad   **b** Internet   **c** je déteste   **d** un appareil photo   **e** barrière

   f J'écoute de la musique en ligne.

   g Tu es accro à la technologie?

   h Alors, quoi de neuf?

   i J'adore jouer à des jeux vidéo en ligne parce que c'est divertissant.

   j Comme c'est informatif, j'aime surfer sur Internet et trouver des sites intéressants.

2 **When speaking French, it is important to think about who you are talking to. Conduct two interviews about use of technology, one with a friend and one with an adult who speaks some French.**

   Use the questions below as a guide and find other ideas in Unit 3.

> **Informal (questions for a friend)**
> Tu es content(e) de ton portable?
> Pourquoi (pas)?
> C'est un smartphone?
> Si oui, qu'est-ce que tu fais avec ton smartphone?
> Quelles activités aimes-tu faire à l'aide des nouvelles technologies? etc.

> **Formal (questions for an adult)**
> Vous êtes content(e) de votre portable? Pourquoi (pas)?
> Est-ce que c'est un smartphone?
> Si oui, qu'est-ce que vous faites avec votre smartphone? etc.

3 **Group work. All around the world, teachers discuss whether pupils should be allowed to use mobile phones in the classroom. What do you think?**

   a Make notes in French about the arguments for and against, in your school.

   b How might the situation be different in an African school, for example in Senegal? Discuss and make notes again.

   c Record or film your group saying their statements. Play the recording back to listen to your progress talking in French about real issues.

Unit 4: Listening strategies

Before you listen:
- Work out the general context. What clues are there in the title? Are there any pictures to help you?
- Look at the task, particularly the questions you need to answer. Think of key words you will need to listen out for, or the types of information required, such as a number, time or price. Predict what might come up.

After you have heard the recording once:
- Be aware: is the recording a dialogue or interview, or is it people talking separately?
- Does the tone of voice of each speaker give any clues?
- Are negative expressions used? If so, focus carefully to understand what is said.

1   **Pair work. Below is a transcript of a recording for a listening task.**

Paul	Je m'appelle Paul. Je dois <u>économiser</u>. Je veux acheter un nouveau portable. Je reçois de l'argent de poche, <u>je reçois 35 euros</u> régulièrement, mais je ne peux pas gérer mon budget. La semaine dernière, j'ai acheté des vêtements. Quand je lave la voiture, Papa me donne cinq euros.
	Bientôt, c'est mon anniversaire. C'est le dix-sept septembre. Maman va organiser un pique-nique à la plage pour mon anniversaire. Elle va prendre des sandwichs, des chips, du chocolat, des fruits et de la limonade. J'espère acheter mon nouveau portable <u>avant le pique-nique</u>!

a   What is the context, i.e. what is it about in general? _____

b   Read the underlined words and phrases out loud to each other.

c   Highlight what you think are the key bits of information that you would concentrate on if you were listening.

d   Be the teacher! What questions could be asked about this listening? Make up five questions in English about it. Supply the answers too.

   1 _____ (Answer _____)
   2 _____ (Answer _____)
   3 _____ (Answer _____)
   4 _____ (Answer _____)
   5 _____ (Answer _____)

2   **Be aware of verb tenses! When an audio extract is about past events, you must expect to hear verbs in the perfect and imperfect tense. If it compares life then and now, it will mix in the present tense.**

		past	present
Read each sentence out loud: does it refer to past or present? Circle the words that give you the clues.	a On faisait les courses avec des francs.	☐	☐
	b On a un lecteur MP4.	☐	☐
	c C'était mieux sans frigos?	☐	☐
	d On n'avait pas de jeux vidéo ou de DVD.	☐	☐
	e Maman, la mode, était-elle importante pour toi?	☐	☐

In Unit 4 you have seen that some changes over time in French-speaking countries are **similar** to changes in your own, while others are **unique** to France.

You have also been thinking about why it is important to keep an open mind. Whatever country you come from, you are well aware that you can learn a lot from studying other cultures.

A deep question for you to consider now: what does it really mean to become **culturally aware**?

Coluche

Michel Colucci (Coluche) rêvait d'un autre monde. Il était généreux et tendre. Il y avait les gens qui avaient faim et froid. En 1985, les Restaurants du Cœur sont nés.

1 **Who or what makes change happen in a country? A well-known comedian, nicknamed Coluche, found something big in French society that he wanted to change. Read the text above and answer the questions. (Use a dictionary if necessary.)**

   a What did he dream of? _____

   b How is he described? _____

   c When was the charity founded? _____

2 **Use the site *www.restosducoeur.org* to find out more about this initiative that has helped, and continues to help, change the lives of poorer people.**

   Follow the link to *www.restosducoeur.org/francemap*.

   a Practise reading out the numbers and places where the restaurants are situated.

   b Use your reading skills to see if you can work out what food is distributed there, and any other details.

   c If you have time, search for the song by Jean-Jacques Goldman, *Les Restos du Cœur*.

3 **Research something that interests you about life in France today, aiming to present some facts as a poster in French. You could research the *Restos du Cœur*, or another topic. Suggestions:**

- the use of English words on French websites
- the popularity of hire bikes in French cities
- the spread of modern tram systems in French cities
- how shop opening hours differ from in the UK
- French comic books – *les BD*.

Prepare your poster, at least A3 size, and be ready to talk about how this research has helped you become more culturally aware.

Unit 5: Checking written work

Always check your written work when you've finished. Use strategies like these from *Allez 1*:
- Take a break after writing your first draft and come back later to **check** it, because you can then look at it in a fresh way.
- Proofread your writing several times looking for **different things** each time. Look at verb endings, verb tenses and adjective agreements, and focus on words that need accents.
- Check all the spelling carefully. If in doubt, **check** in your *Allez 2* textbook or dictionary. This will pay dividends!

New strategies from *Allez 2* to try:
- **Vary** the vocabulary you use, by looking new words up in a dictionary.
- Make your sentences **longer**, using a good range of connectives, such as *donc* and *ensuite*.
- **Divide** your written work into paragraphs, using a table to help you plan.

1 Use a dictionary to find the French for these words. Note whether each one is a noun, a verb or an adjective.

   a handball _____

   b cereals _____

   c to weigh _____

   d mango chutney _____

   e campaign _____

   f rock climber _____

2 Word families. Choose three of the French words you found in exercise 1 and create a mind map for each one, showing words related to it.

3 Read a postcard Marc wrote to describe a meal at a restaurant in Paris. His mistakes are underlined. What corrections are needed? Use a red or blue pen to write in the correct words, letters and accents.

> Salut!
>
> La <u>semain</u> dernière, nous <u>avons</u> allés <u>à la</u> restaurant Dans le noir. C'était <u>l'aniversaire</u> de Sophie.
>
> Elle a choisi un menu surprise. Nous avons <u>mange</u> du poulet avec des frites et du gâteau au chocolat. C'était délicieux mais c'était cher, surtout les <u>boisson</u>. Moi, j'ai bu du coca – 5€!! Une <u>petit</u> bouteille d'eau <u>minerale</u> coûte 7€ et un grand café 4.80€.
>
> Au revoir,
>
>   Marc

Mind map:
- j'aime
- manger
- **les céréales**
- le petit déjeuner

TIP

No one is cross with a toddler who says 'I goed to the park yesterday', because we recognise that they are trying to use the past tense. We expect that as the child grows, they will mimic the sounds they hear and use the correct grammar to say 'I went …'.

4 Write an account of your last visit to a café or restaurant, or an imaginary one. Think of all the strategies you know to help you check your written work, and use them!

In an activity like sport or music, doing your best is all very well but you need to be able to judge **how well you've done** as well. It's the same in learning French. Evaluating your performance and knowing how to do better next time will make it easier for you to control your learning and improve.

Success in music or sport depends partly on **how often** you practise or train. Marathon runners are very aware of their stamina and fitness and how diet contributes to their improvement. So, think about **your routine** learning French and **the diet of French** you have!

Unit 5 mentions 'Frenchness'. Do you want to be able to speak and write French fluently? Listening to French as often as you can will help a lot! What can you do to increase your exposure to French? Maybe switch language on a website you are looking at?

1 **Reflect on how you learn French, using time phrases from page 78 of the Student Book. Be honest about your study habits. Say three phrases in the present tense and one saying what you are going to do to improve.**

Examples: Present: *J'apprends des mots/du vocabulaire une fois par semaine.*
Future: *Je vais écouter du français en ligne deux fois par semaine.*

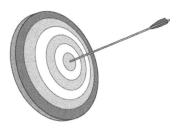

2 **Set yourself some targets for your French learning. Use the phrases in the box and look up any new verbs you need in a dictionary.**

Examples: Il est essentiel de mémoriser les nouvelles listes de vocabulaire.
Je dois utiliser le dictionnaire pour varier mon vocabulaire.

_____

_____

Il faut / Il ne faut pas …
Il est important de …
Il est nécessaire de …
Il est essentiel de …
Je dois …
Je vais continuer à …

3 **Pair work. A challenge to improve your speaking.**

a Without looking anything up, have a conversation for as long as you can, asking each other questions about lifestyle. Look at the Plenary medal tasks on pages 77 and 79. How many minutes can you manage it? Repeat the conversation and record yourselves. Play it back and listen!

Example:
A *Tu manges bien?*
B *Oui, je mange des légumes et des fruits. À mon avis, il est très important de bien manger. Il est essentiel de boire de l'eau. Tu es d'accord?*
A *Oui, il faut boire de l'eau à volonté!*
B *Que fais-tu pour être en forme? Fais-tu du sport? …*

b Reflect on your French. (Discuss this briefly in English.)

- Did you use your bank of questioning words?
- Did your voice go higher at the end of questions?
- How French did you sound? How do you know?
- Which speaking strategies have been most helpful, and what will you try next?

As you get older, you will notice more things that are distinctly **different** about the culture of another country. In spite of the influence of the Internet all around the world, some aspects of life in France just aren't the same as in the UK.

Two key points about French language and culture:

- You will come across colloquial French on websites. In your own mother tongue it's easy to tell the difference between formal and informal language (use of slang and dialect words, for example). See if you can begin to spot this in French too.

- Remember that *vous* is the formal word for 'you' and is used to address someone you do not know well (cashier in a shop, teacher, older people). *Tu* is used to speak to a friend, a member of your family, someone you know well.

1 **Look at the letter and email on page 100 of the Student Book. Remind yourself about differences between formal and informal French. Close the textbook and write whether the following phrases are formal or informal. Highlight the words that give you the clue.**

    a Je vous téléphone demain.   _____

    b Pourriez-vous m'envoyer la liste?   _____

    c Je vais répondre à tes questions.   _____

    d Tu vas bien?   _____

    e Recevez mes sincères salutations.   _____

2 **It is important to know what type of language to use and when. Write a sentence in English explaining why, in your own words.**

_____

3 **Do some independent research on festivals in Europe. Choose an event in an area that you know nothing about before starting. Prepare a poster, Powerpoint, Prezi or storyboard in French about it.**

There are many weblinks, but you could start with this one: *www.europschool.net* and search for *fêtes*.

For example, *Allez 1* featured the *carnaval de Binche*, so you might like to choose another festival in Belgium, such as their *fête nationale* or the Belgian ballooning club at Han-sur-Lesse.

Use all your strategies to prepare a really good presentation and, most important of all, be self-motivated!

Unit 6: Evaluating your and others' performance

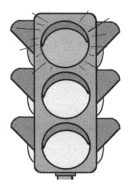

1 What songs or clips from the Internet, or what good apps for a smartphone, can you share with a friend to help them learn? Write the names of at least three.

_____

2 Group work. Imagine you are organising a charity fundraising event. Have a conversation in French, at the planning meeting, to agree who is going to do what and how you can raise funds for the charity of your choice.

- Use the advert below to help you cover all the details.
- Use the key language and the dialogue on page 95, adapting phrases and substituting your own words.
- Try to include all the structures that will make your teacher smile when he/she hears you speak! You must include *on pourrait* + infinitive (see pages 96–97).

Réunion:	samedi prochain à 13h au café en face du collège.
	On va organiser un grand barbecue! Nous voulons collecter des fonds pour les gens qui souffrent de pauvreté. Environ un milliard de personnes dans le monde vivent avec moins d'un euro par jour!
Date et heure:	vendredi 16 juillet, à 19h
Lieu:	terrain de sport
Prix:	5€
Groupes:	1 les courses 2 la musique 3 les grillades

3 Now write a script of the discussion you had in exercise 2. Swap your script with your partner, check the draft and suggest improvements.

4 Time for reflection. What really made you think in Unit 6? What did you find difficult? What is getting easier? Look again at the Unit 6 strategies on pages 95, 97 and 105. What do you think you need to work on most? Jot down some hints for improvement, for yourself and for a partner.

How have you tackled memorising the grammar rules in Unit 7? Did some of the strategies from *Allez 1* help? Keep using the ones that you know help you the most.
- Colour-code the genders of nouns
- Use colour strips for different parts of verbs and for word families.
- Make up a song or rap.
- Create linking maps.
- Be on the lookout for grammatical rules.

New strategies to try:
- Find similarities and differences between French and your first language.
- Make up a story that contains all the exceptions to a new grammar rule.
- Sleep on it! Just before you go to sleep, read out loud the words to remember.

1 **Pair work. Together, colour-code the different tenses in these sentences (present, imperfect, perfect, near future).**

a J'aime prendre le train.

b Mon père m'emmène à l'arrêt de bus en voiture.

c Vous avez des réductions pour les étudiants?

d J'ai passé une semaine en Espagne.

e Je n'ai jamais pris l'avion.

f Il y avait des méduses partout!

2 **Pair work. Take turns to read out the sentences below. Check any tricky pronunciation with your teacher.**

- In each sentence, spot the nouns, verbs, adjectives and adverbs: colour-code them or annotate with **n**, **v**, **adj**, **adv**.
- Then one of you covers them up while the other dictates three sentences to write out. Check the spelling together, then swap roles.

a L'avion est le transport le plus rapide.

b Le vélo est moins polluant que la voiture.

c La voiture électrique est moins polluante que la voiture à essence.

d Quel transport choisissez-vous pour partir en vacances?

e La voiture sera la meilleure solution pour ma famille.

f Si on va en France, on prendra le Shuttle.

3 **Make up a story that uses *-ir* verbs in the present tense (as well as other verbs). Refer to pages 115 and 122 of the Student Book. Write notes, then a first draft, and review it later using your checking strategy to spot any errors you have made.**

Example: Mme Blanc part en Espagne. Elle choisit ...

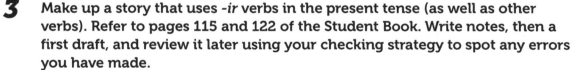

choisir   finir   partir   sortir

In this unit you have started to practise the skill of **transcribing**, starting with *Mes vacances en Corse* on page 117. What is **transcription**? Typically, transcription means **writing** down the **spoken language** you hear, especially in a recording. The tasks below practise this, and build towards transcribing audio statements on page 62 of this Workbook.
Use the Super Strategy of **zooming in**: write down key words you recognise as soon as you hear them, and then focus your attention on the bits you didn't quite get.

1 **Pair work. Watch the phonics video on Kerboodle again and listen carefully to the sounds. Look at the words below. Read out three words each for your partner to transcribe accurately – without looking at them, of course!**

  a l'idée   **b** un innovateur   **c** le métier

  d la chimie   **e** couramment   **f** des risques

  Now read out a phrase each for your partner to listen to and write down:

  a J'ai étudié la physique.   **b** L'entreprise a inventé une nouvelle application.

2 **Pair work. Practise transcribing. Take turns to read out these sentences about transport preferences, while your partner writes them down. Check and analyse together which words were difficult to spell and why.**

  > Moi, je prends le métro ou la voiture pour aller au collège mais j'aime aussi prendre le vélo. C'est plus amusant.

  > Moi, je prends le bus et le vélo tous les jours mais pour aller en vacances, j'aime prendre le train ou l'avion. C'est super rapide!

3 **Pair work. Practise key letter combinations. Spot the spelling pattern in each line, say the words and memorise them.** For example, look at the final letters *-ie* in the country name *l'Algérie*. Listen carefully, and when you hear other words that have this final sound, you will recognise their spelling.

a	l'Algérie	la Normandie	la géographie	Amélie	l'Italie
b	la musique	sympathique	l'océan Pacifique	électronique	la Martinique
c	amusant	marrant	charmant	méchant	malvoyant
d	la nation	la présentation	l'équitation	la natation	l'orientation
e	le dessin	le chemin	le matin	le médecin	la tarte tatin

4 **An extra challenge!**

  a Find three words in the *Allez 2* glossary or in a dictionary that end in *-isme*.

  _____ _____ _____

  b Find as many words as you can that end in *-erie* (clue: types of shop).

  _____ _____ _____

  _____ _____ _____

  _____ _____ _____

Re-read the tip on page 135 of the Student Book about extending your vocabulary. In *Allez 1* you learnt to talk about dream holidays, and now you are learning words related to house-building: what phrases for those topics are in your **long-term memory**, so that you can **retrieve** them and **use** and **adapt** them as your own now?

Just as you save securely the documents on a laptop, or photos on your phone, you must continually save the new words and structures from *Allez 2* in your mind, ready to personalise your work with them.

Being creative with language is the enjoyable part after you have put some hard work into learning.

1 Correct spelling is important when you're being creative. Spot the errors in these phrases and write them out correctly. Use page 147 to help you.

Example: la vie ~~ubaine~~ ⟶ *la vie urbaine*

		incorrect spelling	correct spelling
a	the suburbs of Paris	la banlie de Paris	
b	running water	l'eau courant	
c	recycled materials	des matérials récupérés	
d	electricity	l'electricite	
e	I'd like to build	je voudrait faire construire	
f	the house of my dreams	la mason de mes rêves	

2 Check that you can pronounce the new vocabulary from pages 130, 132 and 134, and can spell all these words correctly.

3 Work on your personal description of *La maison de mes rêves*. Look again at pages 136 (exercise 2) and page 137 (exercise 6). Check that you have mastered all the phrases that relate to your dream house, because they are useful to you. Personalising your descriptions is important. Pages 134–137 include many useful phrases: make language like this your own, by using it frequently!

4 Now work with your partner. You have become the architects of your dreams! Start by saying the title confidently: *La maison de mes rêves*. Describe your dream house to your partner, taking great care with the intonation and pronunciation. Give each other feedback: what should your partner stop and think about in order to improve their French?

5 Creative writing. Choose a form of poem to depict life in a French-speaking country outside Europe. Can you imagine life in one of these countries as a boy or girl of your age? Try to bring in their opinions and feelings too. You can write *j'aimerais …* if you want to imagine yourself there, or write *il/elle aimerait …* to talk about what he/she would like. Use the texts on pages 131 and 137 for ideas.

Unit 8: Translation strategies

> What is **translation**? It involves two languages, unlike **transcription**. Translation is taking the meaning of something in one language and putting it into another language, for example English into French, Arabic into Swahili, German into Finnish. Expert translators are able to express in both languages emotions like happiness or dismay and can match the overall style, such as having a voice of authority. If you read international news you will see examples of this.
>
> Humans are better than computers with the **nuances** of language.
>
> Dictionaries will be useful here, but don't reach for one straightaway. Making intelligent guesses in **context** is a skill to develop first.

1 Translate the sentences into English. Use a dictionary only if absolutely necessary! Check your answers with a partner and analyse together what you found easy and what aspects of translation you need to work on more.

   a Le Bénin est un pays d'Afrique et la capitale est Porto Novo.

   b Au Bénin, on mange souvent des pâtes.

   c Les spécialités sont les boulettes faites avec du maïs, du manioc (= *cassava*) et de la banane.

   d On peux acheter des gâteaux à l'arachide (= *peanut*) et du fromage épicé au marché.

   e On utilise une pirogue pleine de marchandises comme magasin!

2 Translate this blog entry into English, trying to capture Djimon's thoughts.

○○○

Salut!

J'ai treize ans et je m'appelle Djimon. J'habite au Bénin, en Afrique, sur la rivière à Ganvié, à 20 kilomètres de Cotonou. J'y habite depuis onze ans. Mon père m'a souvent dit, 'Le Bénin, c'est la Venise de l'Afrique!'

Ganvié est un village traditionnel de pêcheurs. Nous mangeons du poisson presque tous les jours. Plus de 80% des maisons sont construites sur pilotis. On n'a pas d'espace privé mais je suis content. Heureusement pour notre famille, mes grands-parents habitent ici et nous avons deux pirogues. Le pirogue est le seul moyen de transport dans notre village. La maison de mes rêves? Si j'avais un emploi bien payé plus tard, j'aimerais acheter une maison en bois pour ma famille.

---

la pirogue = *canoe, dugout*
sur pilotis = *on piles, stilts*

3 Group work. Create a freeze frame on an aspect of life in Benin. Try to imagine the life of Djimon and his friends, how they are affected by the weather conditions, feelings, etc. Show them to other groups who describe in French what they see. Discuss which picture is most effective and why:
Moi, j'aime … parce que … Mon freeze frame préféré, c'est …

> The title of spread 9.3 is *Grandes ambitions!* To have them is one thing but to realise them is another. What do successful people have in common? Super Strategies like determination and motivation! The Super Strategies on page 156 will strengthen your motivation and help you learn French.
> Three Don'ts:
> - Don't give up.
> - Don't be afraid to make mistakes.
> - Don't panic.
>
> Two Dos:
> - Do remind yourself regularly what you have achieved so far.
> - Be brave enough to try something you find difficult again, but look for a different way to do it.

1 **a** **Group work. Choose a part and read aloud this transcript of the radio broadcast on page 150 of the Student Book.**

    b **Learn the underlined phrases by heart. Adapt them to personalise your version, and then memorise that. Recording them on your phone is a good first step.**

Intervieweuse	Alors, Sylvie, que voulais-tu faire quand tu étais toute petite?
Sylvie	Je voulais devenir danseuse.
Int.	Et maintenant?
Sylvie	Je crois que <u>j'aimerais être</u> professeur d'anglais parce que les langues sont super importantes. En plus, j'adore les enfants!
Int.	Et toi, Hugo?
Hugo	Moi, quand j'avais dix ans, je rêvais d'être pilote de ligne pour voyager dans le monde entier.
Int.	Et maintenant, tu veux toujours être pilote?
Hugo	Ben, non, pas vraiment ... Maintenant, <u>je préférerais être</u> médecin parce que je voudrais aider les personnes malades et travailler pour une ONG comme Médecins Sans Frontières.
Int.	Et toi, Zinédine?
Zinédine	Moi, avant, je voulais être pâtissier parce que je voulais toujours manger des gâteaux!
Int.	Et maintenant, tu veux toujours devenir pâtissier?
Zinédine	Oui, je veux toujours être pâtissier et <u>je voudrais avoir</u> une grande pâtisserie où je vendrai mes gâteaux!
Int.	Et toi, Anaïs?
Anaïs	Quand j'étais petite, je voulais devenir écrivain comme J. K. Rowling parce que j'adorais *Harry Potter*. Mais maintenant, <u>mon rêve serait d'être</u> dentiste et de travailler dans un cabinet médical!
Int:	Ah, oui, c'est différent! ... Merci à tous et j'espère que vous réaliserez tous vos rêves!

2 **Quiet reflection. Write down in French your own ambitions and your motivation to learn and realise them. Refer to language in Unit 9 if you need to, but try to do this from memory.**

Which strategies promote good speaking and help you prepare for a debate?
- Make the phrases you learn **your own**, by using them frequently.
- Revise phrases for **agreeing and disagreeing** (page 4 of the Student Book).
- If you make a small mistake, **keep going**.
- If you can't think of a French word you need, hesitate and fall back on a **filler word** to 'buy' you some time.
- Listen to effective speakers on TV and radio. Fundraisers, campaigners and many celebrities fight for causes close to their hearts; scientists argue for funds for research. They all **ask** and **answer** questions **confidently**. Copy their example!

As you know, combining **Super Strategies** will help, whatever the task. Below are stages to help you gain confidence with your speaking. Tasks 1 and 2 are working towards a balloon debate in task 3.

1 **Prepare notes on a card about a celebrity of your choice. If it gives confidence, select a few photos too. You can reuse notes from page 149 (exercise 6). Choose a famous person who has been mentioned in *Allez 2* or any other whom you admire.**

2 **Pair work. Practise together, asking each other questions. Use the cards you have prepared. Try to spot the difference between closed and open questions and mix them up to prepare your partner for the group exercise.**

Examples:
Tu as choisi quelle personnalité? Pourquoi?
Décris ta célébrité. Comment s'appelle-t-il/elle?
Où est-il/elle né(e)? Quel âge a-t-il/elle? Où habite-t-il/elle?
Quel métier fait-il/elle? Et quand il/elle était plus jeune, …?

Listen to each other carefully and give support and encouragement. Look again at the tips on pages 149 and 151. Do you need to adjust any of your notes?
Swap partners and talk to another person for two minutes, following the advice your partner gave you. Listen to your new partner.

3 **Group work: Balloon debate.**
- Before the debate, plan in the best French you can achieve. Nominate a speaking expert who is responsible for checking pronunciation. Remind each other about speaking strategies and to watch out for accents.
- Only one of you can stay in the balloon! Who should it be? Take it in turns to be in the hot seat, take on the personality of your choice and convince the others you need saving! Vote to decide who should stay in the balloon! No English is allowed.
- Record your group discussion on a digital voice recorder or mobile phone. Play this back and review your pronunciation afterwards. Discuss strategies for improvement and any problems of pronunciation, noting down individual targets for improvement. Finish with some self-evaluation of your progress in spoken French.

Transcription strategies

On page 57 of this Workbook we started considering what **transcription** is. The skill of accurate transcribing is used in the world of work: legal transcribing takes place in court hearings and at criminal trials, by court officials and reporters; in medical transcribing, a hospital consultant may ask for his/her voice notes to be recorded and transcribed.

Transcription is making an accurate representation in the **same** language, and should not be confused with **translation**, which involves more than one language. Transcribing can be fairly easy if there is only one speaker. If an audio file has more than one speaker, in an interview or group conversation, it can get more difficult. You won't need to do this at a complicated level.

1 **Pair work. Take turns to dictate the following words to each other. Check the spelling.**

    a un appareil photo   **b** surtout   **c** l'ananas   **d** les émissions musicales

2 **Pair work. Choose six more words from *Allez 2* for your partner to write, using the table below. Note the parts of speech in the right-hand column, e.g. noun, verb, adjective, adverb, conjunction, preposition.**

Example: la réalité – noun (F)

a		
b		
c		
d		
e		
f		

3 **Transcribing negative phrases can be tricky. The most familiar ones, like *je ne sais pas,* should be OK, so try to apply a pattern from that if you hear *je ne peux pas, il n'y a pas* and other negative phrases. Dictate these sentences to each other and take turns to transcribe them. Check your spelling.**

    a Il n'y a pas école. C'est un jour férié.

    b Il ne faut pas boire trop de boissons sucrées.

    c Je **n'**ai **jamais** pris l'avion.

    d Ce n'est pas bon pour la santé.

    e Je ne fais pas de sport car c'est trop fatigant.

    f Je **ne** prends **ni** l'avion **ni** le bateau.

4 **Listen again to the statements about famous French people from activity 1 on page 8 of the Student Book. Transcribe each statement as accurately as you can. Compare what you've written with the texts on page 8.**

Coco Chanel   Louis Pasteur